THE EDGE
OF EXPERIENCE

THE EDGE
OF EXPERIENCE

Borderline and Psychosomatic Patients
in Clinical Practice

Edited by

Grigoris Vaslamatzis & Andreas Rabavilas

in collaboration with

R. D. Hinshelwood

London & New York
KARNAC BOOKS

First published in 2001 by
H. Karnac (Books) Ltd.
6 Pembroke Buildings, London NW10 6RE

A subsidiary of Other Press LLC, New York

British Library Cataloguing in Publication Data
A C.I.P. for this book is available from the British Library

 ISBN 1 85575 238 7

10 9 8 7 6 5 4 3 2 1

Edited, designed, and produced by Communication Crafts

www.karnacbooks.com

Printed and bound by Biddles Short Run Books, King's Lynn

CONTENTS

EDITORS AND CONTRIBUTORS

Marilia Aisenstein is a Training Analyst at the Paris Psychoanalytic Society and a Member of the Psychosomatic Institute of Paris. She is also Editor of the *French Review of Psychosomatics*. She has worked for seventeen years in the Association de Santé Mentale du 13ème Arrondissement with psychotic and borderline patients.

Anthony W. Bateman is a Consultant Psychotherapist at St. Ann's Hospital, London, and a Member of the British Psycho-Analytical Society. He is co-author of *Introduction to Psychoanalysis: Contemporary Theory and Practice*.

Peter Hartocollis was Director of the Menninger Memorial Hospital, a Training and Supervising Analyst at the Topeka Institute for Psychoanalysis, and Chairman of Psychiatry at the University of Patras Medical School (in Greece), where he is now Professor Emeritus. He is also Training and Supervising Analyst of the Hellenic Provisional Psychoanalytic Society. He is the author or editor of *Borderline Personality Disorders, Time and Timelessness, The Personal Myth,* and *Introduction to Psychiatry* (in Greek).

R. D. Hinshelwood is Professor of Psychoanalysis at the University of Essex and a Full Member and Training and Supervising Analyst of the British Psycho-Analytical Society. He is author or editor of many books, including *Clinical Klein, A Dictionary of Kleinian Thought,* and *Therapy or Coercion: Does Psychoanalysis Differ from Brainwashing?*

Ilany Kogan is Training Analyst at the Israel Psychoanalytic Society. As a Lecturer and Supervisor at the Tel-Aviv University Medical School, she worked extensively with Holocaust survivors' offspring.

Rafael E. Lopez-Corvo is Training Analyst of the Venezuelan Psychoanalytic Society and author of the books *Self-Envy: Therapy and the Divided Internal World,* and *God Is a Woman.*

Anna Potamianou has a Ph.D. in psychology. She is Training Analyst of the Paris Psychoanalytic Society and of the Hellenic Provisional Psychoanalytic Society and has recently been elected as President of the Hellenic Provisional Psychoanalytic Society. She has published six books and three monographs and has participated in eleven collective publications. She is also a Member of the Psychosomatic Institute of Paris.

Andreas Rabavilas is Professor of Psychiatry at the Athens University Medical School Department of Psychiatry. He has published more than 150 scientific papers and is co-editor of the books *The Treatment of Phobic and Obsessive Compulsive Disorders; Schizophrenia: Recent Biosocial Developments; Psychiatry: A Word Perspective;* and *Current Trends in European Psychotherapy.*

Grigoris Vaslamatzis is Associate Professor of Psychiatry and teaches psychoanalytic theory and therapy at the Department of Psychiatry, Athens University Medical School and at the Hellenic Society of Psychoanalytic Psychotherapy. He has recently been elected as President of the Hellenic Society of Psychoanalytic Psychotherapy. He has published nearly a hundred scientific articles and is co-editor of the books *Countertransference: Theory, Technique, Teaching* and *Current Trends in European Psychotherapy* and author of *The Object of Narcissus* (in Greek).

PREFACE

The practice of psychoanalytic therapy has undoubtedly undergone profound changes over the past two decades. Such changes, mostly concerning the overall technique of the therapy, its eclectic orientation, and its focusing on specific targets, have been brought about mainly by a growing corpus of research on therapeutic outcome as well as the advances made by evaluating the process and, in particular, the therapeutic alliance in treating the "difficult" case.

As far as the latter is concerned, it is of interest to note that most of the psychoanalysts to the First European Conference on Psychotherapy, held in Athens in 1997, whose contributions appear in this book have chosen to deal with problems related to the analysis and treatment of borderline and psychosomatic patients. One may wonder why psychoanalysis is so interested nowadays in such patients. A particular reason has been the change in the type of patients who seek psychoanalytic therapy. The development of psychoanalysis has traditionally been based on "neurotic" patients (usually hysteric, obsessive-compulsive, or depressive) and the classic analytic setting. However, since 1960 there has been a gradual shift in the population who seek psychoanalytic therapy. Patients with a history of trauma, unstable relationships, and chaotic erotic lives, with narcissistic vulnerabilities and psychosomatic symptoms among other problems, now request psychoanalytic help. Heinz Kohut (1977) described this change with the statement that, from a guilt-ridden human being and patient, we are now having to deal with a tragic person (patient).

The development of other psychotherapeutic techniques through which anxious and compulsive patients find alternative therapies and relief might have also contributed to this change, in the sense that such techniques precipitated a novel psychodynamic directivism.

The shift in psychoanalysis from "neurosis" to the "borderline spectrum" proved itself a beneficial process for both sides. These patients were better understood by the therapists and were accepted as clients and analysands. Consequently, the care they were provided with was more effective, regardless of the major difficulties faced when dealing with the integration of their mental structures. On the other hand, psychoanalysis was urged to develop new models for the psyche and the psychoanalytic therapy.

Hence, the theoretical concepts of, for example, primitive object relationships, projective identification, and archaic trauma, among others, were studied and systematized. With regard to diagnosis, useful psychodynamic categories—such as the identity-diffusion syndrome (brought on by the failure to transform infantile indentifications into adult and whole identity) or alexithymia—were introduced and clarified. Finally, with regard to the therapeutic process, countertransference was brought to the foreground of the analysis of the communication between patient and analyst. The new psychotherapeutic paradigm that took shape is, of course, the interplay between transference and countertransference. Also, the importance of the analyst as a new object for the patient is now considered as a therapeutic factor.

Ongoing psychoanalytic research, reflected in current literature regarding the above issues, is plentiful. Our book is a mini-
mal contribution to the clinical understanding and treatment of
borderline and psychosomatic patients from authors who have
been working with them for quite some time. We would like to
thank the psychoanalysts Marilia Aisenstein, Anthony Bateman,
Peter Hartocollis, Ilany Kogan, Rafael Lopez-Corvo, and Anna
Potamianou for submitting their contributions to us and for
their support for the book. Earlier versions of chapters four and
six were published in *Psychoanalytic Quarterly*.

Although we are publishing only a selection of the 1997 conference presentations we would like to thank all the partici-
pants, who greatly contributed to making the conference a
scientific success.

We would also like to warmly thank Professor R. D. Hinshelwood, who read and assisted in the selection of the individual
contributions and commented on them in his Introduction.

Finally, we would like to express our gratitude to Karnac
Books for undertaking to publish this book, thus fulfilling our
endeavour.

Grigoris Vaslamatzis
Andreas Rabavilas

INTRODUCTION

R. D. Hinshelwood

This book of seven papers is a sumptuous meal concocted from the much larger menu at the First European Conference on Psychotherapy, which took place in Athens in the summer of 1997. The organization holding the conference was the Association of European Psychiatrists, and in particular the psychotherapy section of that organization. The gradual convergence of the states of the European Union has promoted such multinational collaboration in all sorts of fields. We must welcome this centripetal force that is bringing psychotherapists together—given the limitless capacity we psychotherapists seem to have to divide and quarrel among ourselves.

Despite this coming together of a variety of therapies, the contributions to this volume come from psychoanalytic psychotherapists. Nevertheless, the work of psychotherapists from different cultures makes a fascinating read, even though it is such a frustratingly brief taste.

It is important that we have been able to publish here two papers from Paris on psychosomatics. The Paris School has made important theoretical advances in understanding the relationship between mind and body. Any such synthesis needs to be reflected in the relationship between psychotherapists and psychiatrists and is a potential meeting point for two professions that in some countries have set up barriers against each other.

The questions that arise from working at this deepest of layers, adjacent to the physical, all gather around the question: how does a mind come about? This is perhaps the most fundamental of all questions for psychotherapists. The move from evacuation and enactment to holding things in mind is a crucial therapeutic step, which the papers by Marilia Aisenstein and Anna Potamianou confront.

Aisenstein claims that the attempt to understand psychosomatic conditions brings the whole of the psychoanalytic project to a completion. This is achieved by the Paris School of Psychosomatics, who argue that what is missing from the psychological world appears in some form in the bodily world. The body is thus a form of language expressing the psychologically inexpressible. This useful rule of thumb leads to a theoretical assumption and a technical innovation—to expand the area of psychological thinking in a patient. Aisenstein calls this a "seduction"—"to induce the patient to discover and share pleasure in psychic functioning".

Potamianou describes a concept from Freud: "indifferent energy". This is the energy left over, as it were, after binding as libidinal or destructive psychic energy. Such remaindered energy can remain meaninglessly attached to the soma. Thus the soma is distinct from the libidinal body (or, rather, the psychically constructed body image). The author then postulates that indifferent energy may be released when the psychic drives become de-fused and when masochism becomes desexualized.

Anthony Bateman in his work with severe and borderline-personality-disordered people also pinpoints the issue of discharge of energy in bodily forms, and the problem of "mentalizing" that ensues. He sets out the theoretical position that underlies the practice of a psychotherapy day hospital that treats these very difficult patients. The chapter starts with a discussion of the nature of acting-out, understanding of which is fundamental to the problems of borderline patients. Enactment is fundamental to their treatment.

Work in a day hospital is not restricted, unlike classical psychoanalysis, to merely verbal behaviour. It acknowledges a world of action or doing that is part of normal life and cannot be excluded from the day hospital setting. That acknowledgement can be the first step towards a communicative process that will bring acting-out to the point of psychological understanding. This is a process that achieves the mentalizing of experience. Bateman's confident theorizing is backed by a quantitative controlled study of outcomes.

Grigoris Vaslamatzis examines in a very detailed and sensitive way the intricate moments when the minds of both the psychotherapist and the patient are processing the experience unconsciously together. The reverie of the psychotherapist is a space in which the patient's inexpressible experiences can rest and survive and reach a new order. It is *in* the therapist's mind that the patient can first achieve experiences not previously tolerated and mentalized. Bion's notion of reverie leads to a close examination of *both* the patient's and the therapist's mental activity. They are intimately linked and in ways that are non-verbal and therefore harder to observe and to think about. A therapist's "involuntary" dream in a session is therefore likely to be connected with the patient's unconscious and projected worries. Such a dream is an example of the therapist having to do the "mentalizing" for the patient—and thus, hopefully, to start off the patient's own ability to expand his or her area of thinking.

Peter Hartocollis, like Bateman, has also struggled gainfully with severe personality disorders, and he has refined a technique that pays careful attention to the immediate here-and-now of the transference. Interpretations focus largely on confrontations with the defensive manoeuvres that go on in the psychoanalysis itself. Since those defences are largely organized around splitting, they result in oscillating changes in the relationship to the analyst—from good to bad and back. That instability can be very provocative to the analyst and be experienced as provocation by the patient. However, these intrusions into the analyst's self-evaluation need empathic understanding of the patient's control of the analyst. Hartocollis also discusses the nature of empathy and considers the current intersubjective school in the United States.

The motivation that brings a patient is often very different from that of the therapist's—the latter's intention is to widen the patient's own mental grasp of his or her experiences. Indeed, it is now well known that the motivation of the most difficult patients is to defeat the therapist—a particularly destructive relationship towards help. Such a negative therapeutic attitude is described by Rafael Lopez-Corvo. He gives some intensely interesting material concerning the internal conflict of a patient in impeding and obstructing him/herself. The female patient whom Lopez-Corvo describes seems determined to thwart any life-enhancing processes within herself. This might be termed a form of self-envy against those aspects of herself that want to develop.

The deadly manifestations described by Lopez-Corvo crop up in another form in Ilany Kogan's work. This chapter is a moving description of the process of an analysis of a patient whose main problem was to experience herself as already dead. The difficulty was not to manage the active deadliness in the patient, as in Lopez-Corvo's patient; rather, it was to cope with the end result of that destructiveness. The patient, feeling already dead, attempted to deal with this defensively with eroticized methods of stimulating a sense of life—especially through homosexual love affairs and by resorting to work in a sex therapy clinic. Kogan argues that the analyst is in a particular kind of conflict with interpretations aimed at the experience that the patient is dead. Then the analyst and the interpretations are experienced as hostile and threatening towards the already "dead" patient. The author found a way through this dilemma by a non-interpretative intervention using a couple of lines from Rilke. The chapter raises very serious questions about being able to analyse such deathly states of mind at all.

We could wonder about these developments—and where they come from. It is perhaps a striking feature of this selection of papers that they are entirely from the psychodynamic psychotherapies, even though non-psychodynamic therapies were represented in the conference in quite a big way. It is true that non-psychodynamic and therefore briefer therapies are able to manage the less severe case. This means that the tough end of psychotherapy is left to the longer-term, psychodynamic therapies. We may be reaching a consensus that these "difficult" patients suffer from excessive hidden and overt destructiveness within themselves. The expression of their destructiveness takes the form of attacking therapy. Perhaps it is only a transference-based therapy that could then really get to grips with such manifestations of destructiveness.

Not only are the non-psychodynamic therapies taking more interest in the here-and-now, but the psychodynamic therapies are themselves becoming more and more focused on ever-finer detail. It seems likely that to take on effectively such difficult patients requires a very careful technique, one that can pick up on the self-defeating quality of the patient's relationships at every minor twist and turn as it appears—hence the close scrutiny of the here-and-now transference that has been emphasized by author after author in this collection.

All the contributions are clinical, intensely so. This focus on clinical phenomena, and how to read them, seems to be a feature of European psychotherapy and of European psychoanalysis. The current emphasis increasingly turns to the intricate subjectivity of psychotherapy itself. Although much is being written about intersubjectivity in the United States, this book demonstrates that the European tradition, which has long taken an interest in plain subjectivity, has still a great deal to teach all of us in this area.

Perhaps the contribution of European psychotherapy as a whole is in addressing the underlying dreams states that lead down to the soma. This book exemplifies this depth of dream-like subjectivity near to the soma, which has preoccupied analysts and therapists the world over.

THE EDGE
OF EXPERIENCE

CHAPTER ONE

Psychoanalytic treatment with psychosomatic patients

Marilia Aisenstein

The question of the psyche–soma is one that has been raised throughout the history of Western thought. Reflecting on thought processes has been one of the fundamental philosophical issues, from Plato to Descartes and on to Heidegger—thought processes that proceed from the body and end with the death of the body.

Various philosophical and theological theories all tend to circumvent the idea that thought is mortal and dependent on the body, assuming instead immortality of the soul, the soul being the centre from which thought is supposed to spring and which is irreducible to the vicissitudes of the body. In this chapter, I offer some semantic considerations and call to mind that, in Ancient Greece, "soma"—the body—did not take on the current meaning of "living organism" until after the fifth century B.C. and Hippocrates. Before the Corpus Hippocraticum became known, the term "soma" referred to the inanimate body, the corpse. Similarly, "psyche" originally meant "breath", and by extension the breath of life and, subsequently, the soul. It is interesting to note that these etymological shifts took place at the time when Hippocrates established medicine as a scientific discipline based on the clinic and on semiology.

Depending on whether the two terms—psyche and soma— are joined or separate, different explanatory systems of man and the world, of life and death, are construed. In a strictly Freudian view, thinking began with the sight of a dead body, a body that was both loved and hated and therefore aroused the double wish: "May he disappear—I want to keep him as he is." This first conflict and its traces convey a part of immortality to thought by giving rise to speculation—which endures longer than the life of a generation—about life and death.

The question of psyche–soma is not a psychoanalytic one: psychoanalysis treats the question and brings a unique and original answer to it. Indeed, in displacing the psyche–soma dualism onto the dualism of the drives, psychoanalysis originates thought processes in this initial conflict. The very definition of drive—psychic treatment of a sexual somatic excitation—confirms, in both drives theories, the psychophysical parallelism that Freud had underscored already in 1891.

The human being is "psychosomatic", and if a thought is also an "act of the flesh", as Tertullianus wrote in the third century A.D., pain and pleasure are also psychic acts. The Freudian description of hallucinatory wish-fulfilment as an expectation and as a distance necessary to the birth of desire testifies to this. Freud does not deal with the field that is today commonly called the psychosomatic clinic—that is, the psychosomatic approach to patients with somatic disorders—but he has laid the bases for it.

In *Beyond the Pleasure Principle* (1920g), in which he introduces the second drive dualism and thus the second topography, Freud distinguishes "pure" traumatisms from those that include organic lesions, and he then notes how the existence of a circumscribed lesion seems to protect the subject against the breaking out of a traumatic neurosis. He also considers the drastic effect of a painful somatic illness on the distribution and modalities of the libido.

The violence of mechanical trauma frees a quantum of excitation that is all the more disorganizing because the subject has
not been prepared by anxiety. On the other hand, the occurrence of a physical lesion may bind excess excitation, because it
calls for a "narcissistic over-investment of the affected organ".
Freud further notes that the pathognomonic mental symptoms
of melancholy or of chronic senile dementia may disappear tem-
porarily in the course of an intercurrent organic illness.

These few concepts from Freud laid, I think, the groundwork
for our own psychosomatic approach.

From its beginnings, the history of psychoanalysis itself has
made it obsolete to retain a restrictive meaning of the two terms
of psyche and soma. Passages from mind to biological body are
not what distinguishes the psychic from the somatic. However,
by opposing sexual drives to instincts of self-preservation—and,
later on, erotic libido to the death instinct—both dualisms put
conflictual investments of the two kinds of drives into dialecti-
cal contradiction.

The Paris Psychosomatic School:
a logical consequence of psychoanalysis

While Hippocratic medicine has laid the foundations for a psychosomatic approach—that is, for an understanding of health in
terms of a somato–psychic equilibrium—the movement embodied in the Paris Psychosomatic School could only have sprung
from the discovery of the psychoanalytic method. I shall not
go into the history of the various successive psychosomatic
theories, but I would like to emphasize that our psychosomatic
practice is fundamentally part of, and results from, psychoanalysis—in fact, in certain ways, it is its acme, its necessary completion.

Freud's remarkable answer to the enigma of the psyche–
soma is that there are not a body and its desires on one side
confronting the psyche and its reasons on the other, but contra-

dictory forces opposing each other in the same somatic field. In "The Psycho-Analytic View of Psychogenic Disturbance of Vision" (1910i), he describes an organ forced to serve two masters at the same time, and he thus gives meaning to the organic symptom. It is interesting to note that, the research model of the time being that of neurosis, and Freud having written very little in terms of psychogenesis, this text has a particular status. In hysterical conversion, the body becomes a language, the symptoms tell an unconscious story, and all mental activity takes its source in the erotic libido. The question of psychogenesis versus organogenesis does, therefore, not seem to be a truly psychoanalytic question. Moreover, to my mind, a strictly aetiological point of view is always reductive. When Freud was confronted with the clinical picture of hysteria, and disregarded the taboo that prevented consideration of the psychic component of certain disorders, he did it in such a way as to illustrate essentially the importance of the sexual in the constitution of the psyche— that is, the body.

Dreams, the *via regia* of the psychoanalytic science, are conceivable only in terms of the clinical aspects of sleep concerning a sleeping subject. Indeed, dreams integrate endogenous and exogenous somatic excitations in an elaborative psychic effort whose first aim is the success of a physiological function: the preservation of sleep. Psychoanalysis is particularly interested in dreams, thus indicating that it takes account of the constant presence of the physical dimension in psychic work. The psychoanalytic treatment of patients suffering from psychosomatic illness constitutes, therefore, a return to the very sources of psychoanalytic thought.

Technical implications of the theoretical model

I shall only briefly mention the theoretical model developed by the Paris Psychosomatic School since 1950. Issues 3 and 4 in 1991 of the *Revue française de psychanalyse* and Pierre Marty's

(1980) work serve as reference in the matter. The basic assumption of the human somato–psychic unity allows us to understand psychic as well as physical phenomena as the sum of dynamic interactions that depend on processes of organization and disorganization. Unless they have a symbolic meaning, somatic disorders are part of a general economy of which the psyche bears witness and which it coordinates.

The great complexity of the psychosomatic clinic is due to the difficulties in assessing, on the basis of psychoanalytic theory, disorders that, as it were, do not correspond to a strictly mental semiology. However, the absence of such disorders is precisely a function of psychic activity. The psychoanalyst–psychosomatician is often confronted with deficient mental organizations, either because this is part of the subject's history or because mental functions are momentarily inhibited as a result of the illness itself and he or she is forced, therefore, to resort to a semiology of *absence*. In doing so, he or she tries to distinguish the habitual factors from the current ones and, for example, to differentiate between absence of conflict linked to deficiencies of the preconscious on the one hand, and a traumatic state, or the use of denial, on the other. Paradoxically, theoretical research cannot in any way adapt to the deficiencies uncovered by clinical investigation, and metapsychological formulations are called for all the more.

This heuristic aspect of the psychosomatic clinic appears to strengthen the interactive links between the theoretical model and practice. We perceive things as a result of our thinkings, yet it is the clinic that inflects our theories and enriches them. A theoretical framework should not be a grid, but a guideline to support elaboration. This point seems *fundamental* to me in *rethinking* a strictly psychoanalytic technique. Precisely in order for it to remain that, it requires particular adjustments and parameters, which I have called here the technical implications of theory.

*Clinical–theoretical parameters
in the treatment of somatic patients*

The currently practised extension of psychoanalytic treatments to patients generally thought of as "difficult cases" allows us all, whether we are psychosomaticians or not, to assert today that we have become familiar with psychic organizations where the original psychoanalytic treatment model proves to be inapplicable as such. Modifying the analytical setting and technique of interpretation to suit the specificity of certain cases does not mean forgoing the rigour of the frame nor the psychoanalytic goal, which is the emergence of transference.

The question is one of choice of method: psychoanalysis, psychoanalytic psychotherapy, psychoanalytic psychodrama, or even psychoanalytic relaxation conducted by a psychoanalyst also trained in relaxation techniques. I shall not expand upon the idea that one needs to be very much a psychoanalyst in order to know when it is necessary to refrain from being one. The practice of psychotherapy requires an extended experience of the practice of classical psychoanalysis. Taking technical liberties implies rigorous reference to the well-internalized model. The wealth of existing literature about this subject speaks to its importance.

However, there are specific problems that one encounters in the psychoanalytic clinic with somatic patients and which I should like to underscore. These are not general factors. Somatic disorders may occur in any given individual, including in persons with highly mentalized neuroses. The psychosomatician is frequently confronted with physical suffering that is neither denied nor particularly invested and may go hand in hand with what seems to be a passive, aconflictual acceptance of treatment. To my mind, these cases are among the most disturbing, and they show the limits of the field of application of psychoanalysis.

I shall come back to the technical implications of the psychotherapeutic treatment of these cases. My first question is: what therapeutic ideal would induce us to propose psychoanalysis to these patients? I do not think that this is a purely ethical question. Symptomatic improvement is a first requirement in psychosomatics, but it cannot be the only goal of our endeavour. It has to be part of a theoretical body based on the founding conviction of man's psyche–soma unity. Our most pragmatic therapeutic choices are based on the assumption of psyche–soma monism and drive dualism, the latter being the source of the essentially conflictual nature of the living—that is, organic—psyche.

Setting up psychotherapeutic treatment presupposes that we adhere to a theory according to which illness and pain are an integral part of a person's mental organization. We propose a course of therapy on the basis of this theoretical conviction, and this implies that we exclude any behaviour that would suggest that the psyche is not a matter of course—that is, that there could be human functions from which the psyche could be absent. Thus, the therapeutic ideal becomes something that one could call a "metapsychological passion", and its very name indicates the psychoanalyst's goal: to awaken a patient's interest in his or her own psychic functioning.

This being said and in order to meet the patient on his or her own grounds—that is, "where he is" at a given moment—a few parameters become necessary that seem to differ from classical psychoanalytic technique. *"What cannot be reached flying, must be reached limping"*, as Freud notes on the last page of *Beyond the Pleasure Principle*, quoting the poet Friedrich Rückert.

In our context, "limping" might be taken as a metaphor meaning the acceptance of a certain adaptive flexibility regarding the patient's affective processes. We must accompany the patient while remaining attentive at all times to the qualitative variations of his or her functioning. This enables us to adjust our attitude. In these cases of extreme narcissistic fragility and frequent lack of interest in the treatment—which is felt to be "endured" passively—interpretations are difficult. Reiterated invitations to associate, however, may foster the emergence of a variety of themes, allowing for the establishment of conversation. I am using this word purposely, because I think that in every psychoanalytic psychotherapy there is this kind of approach, which one might call "an art of conversation" . In order to get the patient interested in thought processes, one must think out loud and solicit him or her. I would not hesitate to speak of a certain kind of seduction that aims at making the patient conscious of the fact that there isn't anybody in the world who has nothing to say, that there is no life without a history, richness, and sufferings, and that there are no stories without words. Apparently aconflictual themes—literature, films, news, and so on—remain intermediaries at first, but they allow us to detect regressive processes and to assess tolerance of excitation and disorganizing effects. Interpretations that I have elsewhere called psychodramatic (Aisenstein, 1991) may sometimes introduce opportunities for identification, while protecting the patients' narcissism. Everything is mobilized to reanimate and sustain preconscious work and to induce the patient to discover and share pleasure in psychic functioning.

I shall quote two brief cases as examples of this long itinerary, including a fragment of a session which has raised questions about the role of interpretation in psychotherapies with somatic patients.

Claire

"Claire", a 32-year-old a chemist, works as a civil servant doing high-level research. Slim and graceful, with regular features and fair hair, she could be attractive but appears somewhat insipid. She dresses plainly; although not really drab, she is, one might say, without radiance. Her muddy, hazy image made me think of an early Odilon Redon painting. She was referred to me by her current cardiologist, who, like his numerous predecessors, was discouraged by the ineffectiveness of the treatment of her apparently uncontrollable, labile arterial hypertension. When she presented herself to me, composed and discreet, I imagined her capable of behaving in a less attractive way, arousing character outbursts in her doctors that the mere unsuccessfulness of the treatment would not explain. There is, indeed, not a hint of querulousness in her discourse. Claire tells her story without sorrow and without humour. She seems not to understand why I should think that she is hurting. She accepts without conviction the proposal of psychotherapy, because although she would like to have a third child, for medical reasons her doctors advise against another pregnancy. Life seems *"empty"* to her; she masters her profession but is not proud of her career. Her parents had suggested to her what she should study; she obtained a degree in pharmacy and, later, the *agrégation* in chemistry, without difficulty but also without passion.

Claire tells me the story of an exemplary existence. She was an only and much-wanted child of an important, well-known couple and went to a private confessional school. Her father was a professor of German studies; her mother had devoted herself to the upbringing of her daughter. Claire's childhood had been a provincial one, with no friends, no going out; her parents had her read, play the piano, go to museums. Spare time and vacations were spent with intensive cultural activities of which Claire seems to have retained nothing, since she is not interested in books or in the arts. Her husband too is a scientist, with a degree from the École Polytechnique. They married young, and two sons were born early on. The boys have developed well. Her parents died five and seven years ago, respectively.

Her hypertension was detected by a school physician when she was 13 years old. Claire has few memories of that morose time, but she recalls having been worried because of pains and tumefactions in her breast. Her mother took her to the family physician, a retired colonel, who seemed most astonished about having to explain to mother and daughter that the latter was beginning her puberty. Claire recounted this episode without amusement and without any criticism of her mother, but she remarked on the disconcerted expression of the doctor. I have often noted her astonishment about people's facial expressions in reaction to her: she is aware of them and worries, but she does not decode them. In my opinion, this indicates an alarming inability to identify with others, and it helps us better to understand Claire's relational difficulties and setbacks. Indeed, her professional/social level and the quality of her vocabulary form a contrast with the preconscious deficiencies that make her prone to projection. To quote an example: at a dinner party, while the discussion was going on about political news, one of her colleagues asked her where she lived; Claire calmly gave her address, and she was believed to be making fun of the person.

This "alexithymia" of self and others, according to the description by Sifneos (1974), is accompanied by a constant wariness and hurt that she does not speak about but I, nevertheless, am aware of. The absence of any playground for identifications combined with extreme narcissistic fragility go, of course, together with the absence of a psychic defence system and present the therapist with major technical difficulties. The necessary confrontation with alterity, through the person of the therapist, calls for a face-to-face therapy to facilitate the work of re-animation and of modulation of the excitations with the aid of proposed figurations. Far from being imposed on the patient in the form of direct interpretations, they may be offered as suggestions and tempered according to the emotional state they provoke. Indeed, encountering the therapist's preconscious elaborations may be an indispensable support for these patients, but there is also the risk that it confronts them with what they experience as their incompletion. A typical phrase like "I still haven't got it" may be followed by an identificatory proposition (in the form of a psychodramatic intervention) like: "Do you think I should feel hurt if I don't get it, if I don't get your equations straight?"

These technical modalities, or particularities, are aimed at affording constant support to the patient's psychic work which is deficient or paralysed, while at the same time they structure the material for a therapeutic process. Little by little a history gets woven that will, in the future, become transferential. At the rhythm of one session per week, over years, the history of Claire's psychotherapy was woven between her and me. While the relationship was being built up, some elements could be brought back into the transference, as, for example, when she told me about a film and I suggested: "Today, you are addressing me saying this. . . ."

Three years passed. Claire had improved symptomatically; hypertensive spurts occurred rarely. She was pleased to come and tried to make connections between thoughts, as well as between the present and the past.

One day, as she told me about her childhood, I was struck by a disturbing absence of representations in myself as I listened to these memories. They were static images with repetitive details. I decided to tell her what I felt, and I said: "I have the impression that you have me turn the pages of an old photograph album." Claire was suddenly very moved and said that when she was little she wondered why there were absolutely no photographs in the house. Shortly thereafter, other forgotten questions came back to mind: her mother had mentioned being born in a town of Eastern France, but she never named the town. At the oral baccalaureate examination, Claire was registered under a double name—her own name, combined with another name that she had never heard. I drew her attention to its Jewish consonance and the fact she was born during the war.

I shall summarize in a few lines the four subsequent years of therapy, which were devoted to the search for her identity and the discovery of her Jewishness. A trip to a distant country, to meet a relative of whom she had known nothing except that he existed, brought to her knowledge the fact that she was really the daughter of the deported brother of the man she considered to be her father. In accordance with Jewish law, the latter had married his brother's pregnant "widow" and recognized the child as his own. They had chosen their French name at the time of their conversion, which had been made necessary by the circumstances. Thrilled by this retrieval of a past that had been covered by silence, Claire became animated, and she read and informed herself in order to catch up with lost time. The analytic work became attractive, associative, more classical. Then Claire decided to have a third child and gave birth to a girl, named Esther. Yet her marriage deteriorated, her husband became a stranger to her, and she no longer knew what to share with him.

A few months later, we entered the third phase of a psychotherapy that lasted eleven years altogether. After a time of elation, Claire became severely depressed. The revival of a mourning process for three parents, which had been blocked and which she had not been aware of, was the positive aspect of this depression, which, however, did not subside and worried me enough to refer her to a colleague-psychiatrist. He prescribed a low dosage of antidepressant medication, which seemed to satisfy Claire so much that she planned never to stop it. At the same time, she told me that her tension had become perfectly normal again without medication. I was intrigued by the simultaneity of depression and symptom relief, and then her cardiologist telephoned me and expressed his perplexity about this astonishing remission in the context of treatment with antidepressant medication. I questioned Claire thoroughly about her bodily and psychic experiences under medication. At this point, she reluctantly revealed to me her old and profound refusal of a feeling of ill-being she had when she was not hypertensed: this impression of limpness and internal flaccidity used to terrify her. Passivity horrified her. In fact, she had taken antidepressants (beta-blockers) only in tiny dosages, fractioning the tablets herself.

During her depression and in spite of the fact that her tension had become low again, the antidepressants gave her a vague feeling of excitement—she called it tonus—that suited her. This admission occurred in the tenth year of treatment and was the beginning of its last phase. The confrontation with her intolerance to passive satisfactions of all kinds threw a new light on her oedipal configuration.

This treatment has been a long adventure made of enthusiastic surges, but also of moments of despair. And I wonder whether such despairing moments would be standable without permanent reference to a theory that sustains the analyst's technical creativity.

Camille

I shall only give a brief fragment of this patient's very different material.

"Camille" has been scarred by analysis. She had been wounded and become mistrustful as a result of a long silent psychoanalysis, which had made her worse. She becomes vindictive and violent quite easily. She frequently had to be taken to intensive care. She knew that she was in danger and she incriminated both the medical science and psychoanalysis. During one of our sessions, she was quite out of breath but, above all, seemed to be tortured by vivid pains; she went pale and took her hand to her heart. I questioned her; she hinted at an uncustomary intercostal pain. At the end of the session, I advised her to see a doctor straight away; three days later she told me that two spontaneously broken ribs had been diagnosed. She said that she would have preferred the pain to be of cardiac origin, because this "break" was like just another humiliation. She then went into a long discourse about the bad effects of cortisone and the shortcomings of Parisian pneumatologists.

At that moment, I have to admit my thoughts had been wandering; a countertransference reaction, no doubt. I had begun to think regretfully of one of my woman friends who had died of the sequelae of an embolism; she had been very slow to begin complaining, as she had thought it to be a broken rib. . . . At that point, I suddenly heard an asthmatic rattle and saw Camille, in a violent rage, heading towards the door. I stood and softly enjoined her to sit down again. I then went on to tell her that she was very angry at me because I had left her for a moment in my mind. In the face of her anguish, I showed her that she had induced my thoughts but that she had, as a matter of fact, remained at the centre of them. Camille calmed down and breathed more easily. I used this moment to make two remarks: I said that it was striking that she could not suffer an absence even for only a fraction of a second, and that I thought that this was rooted in her remote past. And then I seemingly asked myself in her presence: doesn't everyone need psychic space, in someone else's presence, for other ideas to emerge? I said that I believed that this was necessary. However, as the notion of a third party (*tiercéité*) was, at that time, outside Camille's reach, I introduced it in the form of a need of my own, a procedure that, in terms of classical analysis, would be questionable.

I shall forgo relating further details about the work with Camille; instead, I wonder whether atypical interventions like this—which often arise out of an emergency—may qualify as interpretations.

Conclusion:
questions concerning interpretation

I do not call into question the therapeutic value of technical adjustments based on a technical position, but I think that we have to clarify their definitions and their functions.

In principle and strictly speaking, interpretations are aimed at elucidating latent meaning or defensive conflicts. Can this term be retained outside of the classical model—that is, outside of the transference neurosis?

In the psychoanalytic treatment of somatic patients, interpretative interventions often aim at reconstruction, at the unfolding of closely interwoven latent and manifest contents. Is it not antinomic if we call "interpretation" an intervention, albeit a very analytical one, whose function is not to cut across the preconscious but, rather, to sustain a defensive system?

In Serge Viderman's view interpretation not only uncovers but creates a truth. If, indeed, the analytic space we create lies between the preconscious systems of two people, would it not be crazy to assert that we create a durable psychic space within the other person's psyche, a space that will last outside the time and space of the session?

These questions are not purely formal ones; I do not have any certitudes. However (and here we find the theme of drive dualism again, i.e. of the initial conflict), when confronted with difficult patients, the question I have been asking myself is whether an interpretation takes its origin at the meeting point of two contradictory vectors within the analyst.

Words always aim at a resolution, but they also aim at activating the conflict without which psychic life disintegrates. "But why, why are we always in conflict?" one of my analytic patients once said during an analytic session.

Angelus Silesious* [1624–1677] says in "The Cherubinic Pilgrim":

"The rose is without why.
It blossoms because it blossoms"

suggesting that sometimes we have a better grasp of the essence of a phenomenon if we do not search for a motive. I think this is true with regard to the primordial conflictuality (i.e. to the complexity of psychic life): *"why"* may not be a psychoanalytic procedure—but *"how"* is one.

---

*A physician, theologian, philosopher, and poet, born in Breslau, Silesia. His works comprise four volumes, of which "The Cherubinic Pilgrim", written in 1674, is part.

CHAPTER TWO

Sounds of the soma

Anna Potamianou

Illness and somatic disturbances are manifestations of the human psychosomatic unit. In the framework of this unit, psychic and organic phenomena develop in nets of dynamic and economic processes that bear the mark of organization or of disorganization.

Following the Paris School of Psychosomatics (Fain, 1982; Marty, de M'Uzan, & David, 1963), I consider somatic processes to belong to a stream independent of those in which mental phenomena and behavioural manifestations develop. The three orders differ and are autonomous. Consequently, somatic pathology cannot be understood in a direct cause-and-effect relationship with psychic events (e.g. stress, emotional conflicts, archaic fantasies, etc.). In speaking of somatic pathology, I refer to somatization processes that are outside the realm of hysterical conversion or hypochondria and are, in principle, asymbolic, even though they may acquire a symbolic value in the course of psychotherapeutic work.

However, although the Paris School underlines the auton-
omy of the psychic, behavioural, and somatic orders, it does not
exclude certain continuities between levels. Marty (1980) added
also the notion of "complexification"—that is, going from the
more elementary to the more complex forms and articulations in
psychosomatic phenomena, while preserving each level's au-
tonomy and modes of organization, a point that implies also that
of functioning.

I think that for us analysts this view is useful, because it
allows one to envisage possibilities of dynamic integration—or
non-integration—of factors and elements on each level. Leaving
out the idea of causality operating between the somatic and
psychic order, one can start thinking in terms of possible cross-
ings of psychic history with somatic history, asking the crucial
question: "in what context of mental and somatic organization
and of constellation of external events, [is] a movement . . . is
activated that goes towards organic disfunctioning of disease?"
(Dejours, 1994, p. 55).

Psychoanalytic theory has proposed that the energy that is at
the disposal of each psychosomatic unit and that manifests itself
in our sensorimotor activities, as well as in the activity of our
brain and neurosystems (central and autonomous), undergoes a
series of transformations on the psychic level. Coming under the
pleasure–unpleasure principle, the energy qualifies itself as
"drive" energy that uses representations and affects as its representatives.

Through these transformations, brute energy becomes the
psychic potential that makes it possible for us to figurate (i.e. to
transform excitations into images and scene creations); to formulate thoughts and desires or expectations; to cathect mne-
monic traces; and to symbolize and give meaning to what
happens to us, in us and in our world. All this each individual
can experience by observing his or her own mental processes, as
well as those of other individuals during his or her encounters
with them. The individual, then, senses the vibrations of a psychic apparatus that partly contains and partly discharges on the
level of behaviour, of acts, but also of dreams and fantasies the
tensions that mobilize it. In dealing with tensions on the mental

or the behavioural level, our psychic apparatus is constantly engaged in binding/unbinding/rebinding activities.

This type of psychic functioning, although considered to be common, is not always present. Under circumstances of loss, traumatic events, conflictual situations, or failures in primary maternal management, people lose or do not develop the capacity to bind excitations, dealing with them on the mental level. Their defence system is fragile, they often retreat into depression (and depression can start at a very early age), or their mental life gets restricted to everyday operational routines.

Some may perform well professionally and seem to lead a satisfactory family and social life; however, when one hears them talk about themselves, one realizes that their affects and emotions are shallow or suppressed, that splitting mechanisms are in operation, that internalized object relationships are unstable and that diffuse anxieties mark the insufficiencies of the preconscious and of the protective stimulus barrier.

In such cases, ego defences show a poor organization, and even auto-calming behaviour activities—for example, those observed in people who work to exhaustion, who never stop running around, who are given to athletic manias, who are in every sense hyperactive—prove unable to sustain the psychosomatic equilibrium that could serve as a protective shield against the exposure of the psychosomatic unit to excesses of inner or outer stimulations.

Of course, what each psychosomatic unit can deal with differs and can only be evaluated mainly in its after-effects. Somatic illness may be one of these after-effects. But the important question is whether the implied somatic regression will be followed by a reorganization process or, instead, a counter-evolutional disorganization will develop.

This question invites the evaluation of the total psychosomatic economy of each patient, as it suggests that the energy that cannot be absorbed and elaborated mentally may hit the soma.

When the suppression of certain representations and of the affects attached to them impoverishes the capacity of the psychic apparatus to transform and to work through the excitations in ways that allow their mental integration, libidinal cathexis of the body may also suffer from these defects. A delibidinized body is, then, a soma easily exposed to disfunctioning or illness.

Propositions and hypotheses

In trying to deal with internal and external stimulations, the ego uses various means to negotiate and treat excitations. Yet, as every clinician knows, we often come across patients for whom the working through of tension produced by inner or outer stimuli is not an easy task. This often proves to be the result of early traumatic experiences during which primary and secondary thought processes were flooded by excesses of excitations; what we observe later is the after-effect of what occurred during a critical phase of life, often on an already sensitive ground. Reactivation of traumatic situations may lead to compulsive repetitions, behaviour manifestations, acting-out, or implosions in the soma whenever the ego is unable to supply firm lines of countercathexes around, and on, the margins of the traumatic breach. Overloaded with excitations, the psychic apparatus cannot continue to maintain the pleasure principle in action (Freud, 1920g, p. 29).

In cases where narcissistic pathology predominates, countercathexes—fuelled primarily by narcissistic libido—make powerful demands in terms of energy concentration. However, they are often not dense enough to yield a substantial fabric. In that case, they cannot form the regulating screen whereby repression and ego homeostasis can be preserved, or they may nurture grim resistances that serve for a while but are not immune to inside or outside storms. The patients are unable to restrain, and to work on, the clamorous productions of the unconscious when such productions emerge on the psychic scene. Occasional or permanent deficiencies of the binding capacities of the preconscious, as well as failures of erogenous masochism, are holding the ground.

In severe psychosomatic pathology, we may find that the eroticized masochism is in recession, if not completely neutralized. Cathexes of excitation per se and evacuation/discharge processes prevail, while auto-destructiveness bears the sign of very low drive mixing, thus leaving both the psychic organ and the soma unprotected. This failure, or degradation, of the masochistic component joins the concept of lethal masochism (Rosenberg, 1991). As a matter of fact, one could say that the term "masochism" should be used in such cases only in order to point out the masochistic disorganization and the defects of the primary masochistic kernel that leads to unbound destructiveness invading the psychic realm, as Freud (1933a, p. 109; 1937c, pp. 242–243) pointed out.

In this framework, temporary or permanent decathexes of object and of ego functions can be understood as the result of drive unmixing. Deficiencies in binding between derivatives of the aggressive and erotic drives encourage the development of auto-destructiveness, thereby neutralizing the synthetic function of the ego, blocking internalizations, differentiations, and modulation of affects, and impeding the oscillatory movement of cathexes–decathexes and recathexes.

This set of problems calls into question defects of the external protective shield (role of the object), as well as of the internal protective shield (system of defences), while drive unmixing—evident in unmitigated destructive manifestations and/or massive, uncontrolled, or rigidly fixed libidinal cathexes—gives free rein to regressive motions.

Regression may go far back on the scale of mental fixations, and it often leaves the latter well behind. In this case, the soma implicated in the process is no longer a libidinal body.

But one question still remains open: that of the destiny of the energy liberated by decathexes. Is it implicated in somatic illness? If so, in what ways? In trying to answer this question, I shall present some propositions I made some time ago (Potamianou, 1994).

In his text "On Narcissism: An Introduction" (1914c, p. 78), Freud introduced the idea of an "indifferent" psychic energy (indifferent, not "neutral" as it was translated into French and in some English texts). He said that it is transformed into libido only when it cathects an object or the ego.

In *The Ego and the Id* (1923b, p. 44), Freud again took up the concept of "indifferent" energy and affirmed that it is displaceable and can be added to the energy that is differentiated by its erotic and destructive qualifications and reinforces it. The energy is transformed into libidinal or aggressive drive urges when it gets bound to objects and comes under the aegis of the pleasure–unpleasure principle. This is the process of transformation of the brute energy into a psychic force.

One must add that Freud spoke also of the action of energy motions that he calls "psychical representatives", motions that are not yet linked to the representations/representatives or to affects.

What is assumed, then, is that the energy manifest in the capacity of our body to get stimulated is that which is transformed into psychic energy; it operates according to the pleasure principle, finding its qualifications while cathecting erotically or aggressively the objects and when attached to its representatives (representations and affects).

Freud is, thus, I think, calling our attention to the process of passing over from the somatic to the psychic level.

The term "indifferent energy", which relates to the idea of an unspecified energy, underlines: (1) the notion of "drive" as a "boundary" concept; (2) the idea of transformations in energy, from the somatic force that produces rough, brute, excitations to its potential changes on the psychic level; and (3) that the term "indifferent" also designates a remainder—not only a remainder available for the establishment of links, but also one that can resist psychic transformations. This implies that "indifferent energy" is not necessarily related to the drive set up (urge–object–aim).

What, then, is the destiny of this force that resists psychic qualification? And what happens when libido gets disqualified at times of drive unmixing and masochistic dis-erotization?

Discussion

If we accept that the indifferent and displaceable energy can add itself to the energy qualified as erotic or destructive in order to reinforce it, the contrary movement is conceivable as well.

When the psychic apparatus is exposed to excesses of excitations that surpass its capacity to negotiate them, movements of unbinding on the mental and the behavioural levels, as well as motions of drive unmixing, may result (Potamianou, 1997). Such movements indicate that something cannot be elaborated on the psychic level; they also indicate that the apparatus can be invaded by auto-destructiveness, as Freud (1937c) stated: "One . . ., free force . . . only a portion of it which is, as it were, psychically bound by the Supergo and thus becomes recognizable; other quotas of the same force, whether bound or free, may be at work in other, unspecified places" (pp. 242–243).

The disorganization of the masochistic component leads to situations where unbound drive motions lose their erotic or aggressive libidinal qualifications. These drive charges are reabsorbed in the flow of indifferent energy.

Along that line of thinking, I consider that the concept of "indifferent energy" can be used as a metaphor that indicates the passing over from somatic energy to its psychic qualification as "drive" force, or, in the opposite direction, it refers to what goes back to the non-physically qualified somatic charges.

The trace of this reverse movement is hinted at by Freud in *An Outline of Psycho-Analysis* (1940a [1938], p. 199), where he says that an excess of external or internal simulations can again change the ego into a part of the id. About the id he says (p. 148) that not only does it not care to protect itself from dangers through signals of anxiety, but that it does not even turn its attention towards survival.

With the id remaining in its depth open to the soma (31st Conference of the International Psychoanalytic Association), the sources of energy being somatic and the progressive integrative movement of the ego being impeded, we can understand that the increase of indifferent energy may favour somatic discharge.

Somatic symptomatology or illness can then serve to tie on the soma those energy charges that escape binding on the psychic level.

Following this line of thinking, I propose to consider somatic illness as a sound emitted by the psychosomatic unit. On the mental realm, a sound can have a symbolic meaning as well as a value of communication. On the organic level, emitted by a body that functions outside the realm of hysterical or hypochondrial preoccupations, sounds may only secondarily acquire a symbolic meaning through the psychotherapeutic endeavours.

But why, then, should one place somatic pathological symptomatology in the category of sounds? The answer I can give is that it seems important to consider these symptoms as signifiers—that is, to endow them with a dynamism able to call the attention of doctors and psychotherapists to the need of being sensitive to the differences in tunes which indicate psychosomatic crises, leading along the path of regression–reorganization or of counter-evolutional disorganization.

CHAPTER THREE

Day hospital treatment of borderline personality disorder and the containment of enactment

Anthony W. Bateman

The term "borderline personality disorder" (BPD) has emerged from a confluence of psychiatric and psychoanalytic research. From a psychiatric point of view, the DSM-IV descriptive criteria for a diagnosis of BPD can be summarized as "stable instability", comprising intense but unstable interpersonal relationships; self-destructiveness; constant efforts to avoid real or imagined abandonment; chronic dysphoria such as anger, boredom, or depression; transient psychotic episodes or cognitive distortions; impulsivity; poor social adaptation; and identity disturbance. Not surprisingly, such patients present frequently to psychiatrists, and they represent 11% of all out-patients and 19% of in-patients. Medication alone is an inadequate treatment (Soloff, 1998), and psychiatrists frequently refer borderline patients to psychotherapists.

From a psychoanalytic perspective, BPD has evoked intense theorizing among psychoanalysts and, perhaps because of its clinical difficulty and variability, represents a battlefield upon which many of the controversies and schisms of contemporary psychoanalysis have been played out. The main difference is between authors who emphasize conflict and those who stress deficit as the central psychopathological theme, each group advocating apparently very different treatment approaches. The "conflict" group includes both the classical Freudians—and neoclassical Lacanians—and the Kleinians and their followers, while the "deficit" group comprises, in Britain, the Independents and, in the United States, the Interpersonalists and Self psychologists. In practice this divide is somewhat artificial, and the evidence suggests that both conflict and deficit are important in the aetiology of BPD, that both intrapsychic and environmental factors play an important part, and that different authors are probably describing and treating different patient populations with different clinical needs. Borderline patients are a heterogeneous group and vary in the severity of their psychiatric symptoms, their suicide risk, and their propensity to self-harm, as well as in their degree of chaotic and impulsive behaviour. Thus, classical out-patient psychoanalysis may be inadequate and psychoanalytic treatment may need to take place in an in-patient (Norton & Hinshelwood, 1996) or a day patient setting and be followed by out-patient and community work.

Whatever theoretical psychoanalytic view is taken and whatever the context of treatment, most authors agree that enactment of conflict between patient and therapist is inevitable and may be to either the benefit or the detriment of treatment.

Enactment

Enactment is a hybrid term incorporating ideas commonly subsumed under acting-out, acting-in, actualization, repetition, transference, and countertransference. There is no universally agreed definition of the concept, which leads to the danger that it is meaningless and adds little to our attempts to refine analytic theory and to understand our patients better. Nonetheless, there are two main themes running through the literature on enactment.

First, enactment is considered to be an interpersonal phenomenon, involving action of variable severity between patient and analyst. At the benign end of the spectrum, enactment is equivalent to an "actualization" (Sandler, 1976a, 1976b) between patient and analyst of a patient's wished-for transference relationship. At the more severe end of the spectrum, the analyst's objective capacities are compromised and both analyst and patient jointly overstep a boundary. Mclaughlin (1991), Chused (1991), and Roughton (1993) follow this view, distinguishing enactment from acting-out on the basis of the contribution from the analyst. Enactment involves the analyst as participant, vulnerable to his or her own transferences, susceptible to "blind spots", and caught up in the relationship rather than alongside it, whereas acting-out implicates the analyst solely as an observer.

Second, there is a theme of enactment as a positive force in treatment, even to the extent of suggesting that it may form part of a "corrective emotional experience" (Roughton, 1993). Following enactment, the analyst extricates himself, separates his own conflictual participation from that of his patient, and guards against becoming self-punitive about his failure to maintain neutrality, thereby enabling the enactment to lead to understanding and progress. However, this is not inevitably the case, and enactments are equally likely to lead to a breakdown in treatment if a therapist is not helped to understand the meaning of his or her countertransference response either through personal therapy or through supervision and case discussion.

It is this author's view that careful consideration needs to be given both to the conflict and deficit models of BPD and to the transference/countertransference matrix if treatment is to be effective, breakdown of therapy is to be avoided, and enactments between staff and patients are to be minimized.

In this chapter, I describe a psychoanalytically orientated day hospital programme for patients with severe BPD whose difficulties make them impossible to treat within a "classical" psychoanalytic model. The day hospital programme takes into account both conflict and deficit models and emphasizes staff discussion of countertransference responses, in order to avoid excessive enactment. The programme has been evaluated in a randomized control trial. The results, which are promising, are summarized in the final section.

Day hospital programme

The day hospital programme involves two stages. The first stage is treatment in a day hospital for a period of eighteen months. This is followed in the second stage by follow-up treatment of twice-weekly out-patient group psychotherapy for a period of up to four years.

There are four areas of psychoanalytic theory that are helpful in thinking about a psychoanalytically orientated day hospital treatment programme:

1. the therapeutic alliance;
2. the type of interventions;
3. the triangulation of relationships to encourage the development of a mentalizing capacity;
4. the containment of countertransference responses of staff, to prevent enactments that lead to breakdown in treatment.

Therapeutic alliance

Drop-out rates are high during the treatment of borderline patients (Gunderson et al., 1989). Patients show marked oscillations in attachment. On the one hand, they become highly dependent, seeking protection from abandonment; yet, on the other, they become terrified of loss of identity and take flight. An oscillating attacking and clinging relationship develops that threatens the stability of treatment and precipitates crises in which the patient experiences the treatment setting as failing him or her. On occasions, there is an actual failure of treatment,

such as an inappropriate intervention, and this should be acknowledged. But, more often, crises are a recreation of chaotic
and unsatisfactory relationships of the past, since the unconscious seeking of aggressively charged, chaotic relationships
and repetition of negative affects preserves for the borderline
patient a maladaptive sense of security, a cohesion of a fragile
sense of self, and an optimal level of familiar feeling. Intervention threatens this psychic adaptation, frequently leading to a
breakdown of treatment. This pattern can be overcome in a day
hospital programme.

A long period of engagement of the patient in treatment
needs to be undertaken, up to perhaps three months. A drop-in
facility exists for patients, and home visits may be necessary. A
major aim of this aspect of treatment is to foster a sense that the
unit is a place in which staff and others try to understand rather
than to judge, to talk rather than to act, and to tolerate instead of
reject. It is the beginning of a therapeutic alliance, an alliance
that needs to be fostered throughout treatment. In this way, a
patient develops a relationship that becomes more and more
real rather than it being a vehicle for projections and preconcep-
tions.

Type of intervention

Winnicott, in a chapter in *Playing and Reality* (1971) on creativity
and its origins, writes about the capacity to be, or "being", and
contrasts it with an active manner of object-relating, or "doing".
He equates "being with the object" with the more receptive
female element and "doing something to the object" with the
more active male element, both elements being potentially
present in every man and every woman. Wolff (1971) has put it
differently, as "being with" and "doing to". Wolff suggests that
"being with" involves a high degree of empathy and sensitivity
to what the patient is experiencing. In contrast, "doing to" is
more concerned with outward behaviour rather than with its
inner meaning, and, correspondingly, therapists use their critical and intellectual functions more than their intuition and feel-

ing functions. It is probably true to say that this balance alters in any treatment, and the art of dynamic therapy consists of finding the right balance between "being with" and "doing to". In fact, the "doing-to" functions very often require a well-established "being-with" relationship before they become effective. How is "doing to" and "being with" translated into a day hospital programme?

For a start, the programme is divided into two parts—a morning session and afternoon session—representing, at a superficial level, a differentiation between "being with" and "doing to". In the mornings, both small and large analytic groups are held; small groups occur three times a week, large groups twice a week. Group psychotherapy acts as a potential space into which patients project aspects of their inner world. Projection into a potential space faces the borderline patient with his or her greatest fears of annihilation, emptiness, and boredom. Consequently, these affects and their expression within the analytic groups form the focus for both patients and therapists. Interpretation—a "doing-to" function—is used, but an emphasis on empathic understanding within a secure, non-directive milieu means that "being-with" interventions predominate. But too much space stimulates annihilation anxiety and regression, leading to impulsive self-destructive acts. In order to counterbalance this danger, the afternoon programme comprises groups consisting of art therapy, psychodrama, writing, and relaxation therapy. These structured and problem-orientated groups take place once-weekly and are carefully linked to the analytic groups to ensure continuity of themes. For example, if abandonment is a major theme in group analysis, the structured groups will focus on abandonment, explore ways of expressing the feelings through a different medium, and identify ways of coping. Thus, although there is a mix of "doing-to" and "being-with" interventions in the afternoon groups, therapists take an expert "doing-to" role rather than a facilitative, "being-with" function. In between group therapy, there is free time to allow self-reflection, peer support, and patient interaction without staff intrusion. Other aspects of "doing to" and "being with" in the day hospital programme have been described elsewhere (Bateman, 1995)

Triangulation of relationships

Fonagy (1991) has suggested that the borderline experience can be understood in terms of a lack of mentalizing capacity. A lack of mentalization leads to an inability within a person to think about thinking or to understand the mind of others, thereby finding it difficult to accept individual differences in emotions and perceptions. Such a capacity can develop only if a child has the experience of being seen as a separate person, with his or her own thoughts and feelings—a type of validation. In the context of psychological development, such a spatial process requires an internalization of a "third" point of view, a father if you like, from which a child can reflect on him/herself in relation to others. Such a process is inherent in group psychotherapy, but to focus it further each patient has an individual session once a week. Thus, there is a place for the patient to think about him/ herself in relation to the rest of the treatment programme. Furthermore, the practical and social aspects of each patient's programme are separated from the role of the therapist. The therapist is left to get on with therapy while his or her patient's other needs, such as medication, social benefits, college reports, and so on are dealt with elsewhere—a triangulation between the patient and members of staff.

Failure to "mentalize" results in enactment if frustration builds up in both patient and therapist. Yet not all actions in a day hospital setting are enactment, because the golden analytic rule of "verbal interaction only" has to be relaxed within a therapeutic milieu. Patients are responsible for each other and take an active role in maintaining boundaries of a programme, as this aspect is not left to the therapists alone. A patient who seeks out another who is absent from a group, tells the person firmly to attend, and forces that person into the group room may not be failing to mentalize; he or she may have realized that the continuity of the group is compromised and that conflicts remain unaddressed due to absence. Alternatively, a patient who threatens physical force against a patient who is absent may just be engaged in an action to dominate and may be failing to think about his or her underlying frustrations. Careful teasing out of underlying motivation is helpful in distinguishing mentalized and non-mentalized actions.

Failure to mentalize results in excessive splitting and projection. Borderline patients evoke different responses in different staff, leading to schisms and unhelpful polarization within a staff group. How staff react to these differences is crucial to the development within a borderline patient of a capacity to think and to tolerate uncertainty and difference. Consequently, arrangements for supervision and staff meetings are paramount. Staff meet after each group to "metabolize" the emotional responses engendered so that the intrapsychic splits so commonly found in BPD are not realized within the staff group through the enactment of split transferences. Differences need to be expressed and challenged within a cohesive staff team so that contradictory views are integrated, reformulated, and used constructively in treatment.

Containment of countertransference

Unstable interpersonal relationships are the hallmark of BPD. Repetition of former patterns of behaviour occur during treatment through transference and countertransference. A therapist has carefully to monitor his or her own emotional reactions to avoid being drawn into constant battles, to prevent being enticed into endless justifications of an action or interpretation, and to circumvent being induced to act outside the therapeutic relationship. The capacity of the therapist to survive and to continue thinking under such circumstances is vital to the success of any treatment.

In order to ensure optimal processing of countertransference responses, we attend carefully to the emotional and physical safety of staff. In addition to personal therapy, the key is the development of a cohesive staff team capable of maintaining a structured and secure base for treatment. The rapidly alternating projective systems so commonly found in borderline patients potentially "drive staff mad", leaving them unable to think clearly and prone to enactments infused with hatred of patients. Each day, staff meet together to discuss the form and content of groups and individual sessions. In this way, staff learn from each other and attempt to integrate different aspects of a patient into a coherent whole. The staff group represents, within the day hospital, a process of thinking about thinking.

Mood and behavioural fluctuations of patients are dealt with by structure and containment along with a non-anxious attitude of staff to crises, acute acting-out, and persistent provocation. Structure is maintained through adherence to a treatment milieu; containment is maintained through interpretation and by offering twenty-four-hour contact at times of crisis. A calm and thoughtful demeanour on the part of the therapist is established by supervision, by working within a specialist team, and by understanding one's own reactions better through personal therapy.

Overall, the programme comprises a stable framework; a maintenance of a therapeutic milieu; some limit-setting; an interpretative focus on understanding the here-and-now, with a balance of "doing to" and "being with"; containment of aggression and self-damaging behaviour by firm, non-punitive handling; constant reflection on countertransference reactions; and attention to social problems through task-orientated groups.

Aims of treatment

The aims of our treatment programme reflect both the therapeutic and the management difficulties of the borderline patient, with an emphasis on relational aspects of the disorder. They are as follows: (1) to engage the patient in treatment, since drop-out rates are high; (2) to reduce general psychiatric symptoms, particularly those of depression and anxiety; (3) to decrease self-destructive acts and suicide attempts; (4) to improve social and interpersonal function; (5) to prevent reliance on hospital admission in a crisis; and (6) to bring about permanent changes in an individual's personality and internal world in order to promote lasting psychological maturation.

Treatment outcome

Full details of the design of the study and outcome of treatment may be found elsewhere (Bateman, 1995; Fonagy, 1996); only an outline is given here. In a randomized controlled design, borderline patients were assigned (for a period of eighteen months) either to intensive treatment in the day hospital programme or to treatment-as-usual in the general psychiatric service. Treatment-as-usual in the general psychiatric service was chosen as the approach to control for spontaneous remission; patients were able to participate in normal psychiatric treatment, seeing their doctors and nurses when necessary and receiving general psychiatric day hospital treatment (72%), out-patient and community follow-up (100%), and in-patient admission (90%) as appropriate. The general psychiatric day hospital treatment involved an occupational therapy programme incorporating art therapy and music therapy, but none of the control group received any formal psychotherapy. While the control group cannot be considered to have received a comparable amount of professional attention to that of the intensive-treatment group, the control is valuable from the point of view of the effects of medication as well as spontaneous changes in mental state.

Patients entering the study were assessed at entry with a structured interview, the SCID-1 and SCID-2 (Derogatis, 1983). Depression and anxiety were measured using the Beck Depression Inventory (BDI: Beck, Ward, Mendelson, Mock, & Erlbaugh, 1961) and the Spielberger State–Trait Anxiety Inventory (Spielberger, Gorsuch, & Lushene, 1970), respectively. In order to ensure assessment of areas targeted by psychoanalytic therapy, social adjustment and interpersonal function were measured pre- and post-trial using the modified Social Adjustment Scale self-report (SAS-M: Cooper, Osborn, Gath, & Feggetter, 1982) and the Inventory of Interpersonal Problems—circumflex version (IIP: Alden, Wiggins, & Pincus, 1990; Horowitz, Rosenbery, Baer, Ureno, & Villasenor, 1988). These provide an assessment of an individual's work, spare-time activities, family life, and difficulties with interpersonal function. The reliability and validity of all these instruments is well established.

Monitoring of symptoms during treatment was with self-rating questionnaires at three-monthly intervals on all symptom measures, with the exception of the SCL-90-R (Derogatis, 1983) which was given at six-monthly intervals.

Clinical measures included number of hospital admissions and length of stay, and number of suicide attempts and acts of self-mutilation. For all patients, a search of the hospital in-patient database was made to obtain the number of hospital admissions and length of stay during a period of six months prior to entry into the study. This was cross-checked with the medical notes. Hospital admission and length of stay and psychiatric day hospital programme attendances were monitored throughout the study for all patients.

The criteria for suicidal acts were: (1) deliberate; (2) life threatening; (3) had resulted in medical intervention; (4) medical assessment was consistent with a suicide attempt. Criteria for acts of self-mutilation were: (1) deliberate; (2) resulting in visible tissue damage; (3) nursing or medical intervention required. A semi-structured interview (Suicide and Self-harm Inventory) was used to obtain details of both suicidal and self-damaging acts for the six-month period before patients entered the study. This interview asks specific questions not only about numbers of acts but also about dangerousness of acts (i.e. presence or absence of another person, likelihood of being found, preparation, and lethality); multiple acts over a short period of time—for example, a frenzied self-cutting—were counted as a single act. Day hospital patients were monitored carefully with regard to self-destructive acts, and control patients were interviewed every six months. Self-reports of suicidal and self-mutilatory acts were cross-checked with medical and psychiatric notes.

Twenty-five patients with BPD were treated with a psycho-analytically orientated day hospital programme and compared with nineteen patients treated with standard psychiatric care. In contrast to the patients treated within the general psychiatric service, who showed little change or deterioration, the patients treated with the day hospital programme for eighteen months showed significant improvement on both symptomatic and clinical measures. Particularly notable was improvement in depressive symptoms, decrease in suicidal and self-mutilatory acts, reduced in-patient psychiatric days, and better social and interpersonal function—which is an area specifically targeted in psychoanalytic psychotherapy. Treatment was effective both for males and for females. Improvement in psychiatric symptoms and suicidal acts occurred after six months, but a reduction in frequency of hospital admission and length of in-patient stay was only clear in the last six months, indicating a need for longer-term treatment. No patients committed suicide.

It has been mentioned that a major effort is made to ensure that destructive enactments within the transference–coun-tertransference relationship are minimized. The reduction in self-damaging acts suggests that this therapeutic aim was successfully realized. Individual sessions focus on the meaning of such acts as understood within the context of the therapeutic relationship. For example, some patients are more likely to harm themselves at the time of a therapist's absence, and so this is interpreted. Further evidence for the success of containing destructive enactments comes from the fact that the programme and staff were effective in retaining patients in treatment. This is in contrast to in-patient and out-patient psychoanalytic treatments for BPD (Gunderson, Kolb, & Austin, 1989; Waldinger & Gunderson, 1984). Only three out of twenty-five (12%) patients dropped out of the programme and could not be re-engaged. There are a number of possible reasons for this. In the first place, the structured nature of the programme ensures that patients are fully aware of the boundaries of treatment. No formal contract was made, as experience suggests that borderline patients unwittingly sabotage their treatment. Discharge due to failure to meet stringent attendance requirements is likely traumatically to re-enact the abandonment that the borderline patient is both desperate to avoid but simultaneously provokes. Second treatment within a day hospital programme simultaneously balances support and treatment with separation and individuation. This mirrors the central conflict of the borderline patient, who eschews excessive intimacy and yet fears abandonment. The programme is neither too much nor too little. This contrasts both with in-patient treatment, which may stimulate loss of identity and terror of entrapment, and with out-patient treatment, which may evoke overwhelming feelings of abandonment. Third, there is active pursuit of non-attendees by phone, letter, and home visit if necessary. Finally, the factors leading to non-attendance are worked through within the transference–countertransference matrix of individual therapy and their meaning understood.

The patients in this study represent a severe group of BPD. They were of mixed sex, showed severe levels of depression, suffered from high levels of symptomatic distress, and demonstrated co-morbidity especially for affective disorders. Alleviation of depression may have been a result of antidepressant medication. However, this explanation seems unlikely since the patients within the general psychiatric service received higher doses of medication for longer and improvement occurred later than would have been expected with antidepressants. Amelioration of depressive symptoms may be understood from a psychoanalytic viewpoint as a result of the development of a stable soothing introject and better attachment representations, with associated improvement to negotiate separation.

It remains unclear whether the gains will be maintained over time, although a follow-up study is in progress. The day hospital team is enthusiastic in the treatment of BPD and shows strong allegiance to a psychoanalytic approach, and this may have influenced self-report outcome. It is possible that the amount of staff time received by the day hospital patients is responsible for the improvement; however, the control group also received large amounts of time themselves through hospi-

tal admission and day hospital treatment, so this seems unlikely.

This was not a study specifically looking at cost-effective-
ness, and there are no detailed data to provide exact cost differences between the two groups. Offering borderline patients an
intensive day hospital programme may seem too much, but
offering a less structured and less intensive programme is inadequate and fails to reduce the medical risk of suicide, decrease
the number of hospital admissions and length of stay, and di-
minish symptoms. There are obvious economic advantages in
minimizing recourse to expensive medical treatment following
overdose and avoiding prolonged hospital admission. Shorter
stay in hospital for the day hospital group cannot simply be
because this group had a programme to which they could return. All in-patients within the psychiatric service are discharged to a general psychiatric day hospital programme for a
variable length of time agreed between patient and psychiatrist.

It is clear that the psychoanalytically orientated programme
shows a treatment effect. It remains unclear which aspects of the
programme are essential for progress, particularly since the
control group received a treatment package that included day
hospital care and extensive out-patient support as well as in-
patient care; however, this lacked coherence and was inconsist-
ently applied, particularly at times of crisis. It is likely that a
multi-component programme is necessary and that the critical
feature is the way that its components are brought together.
Dismantling studies looking at the necessity of different aspects
of a treatment package are possible, and it would be of interest
to determine whether both interpretative and expressive therapies are necessary or whether one component alone is adequate.
But such studies are difficult, and it may be more important to
determine whether eighteen months of treatment is required or
whether a shorter time would be equally beneficial. In my view,
essential features of an effective programme include a theoreti-
cally coherent treatment approach involving a relationship focus that is consistently applied over a period of time. Under
these circumstances, not only is there a structured treatment
plan with clear boundaries but also a focus for the mind of the

patient, allowing transferences to be concentrated rather than being split between different staff of a large service and between various clinics, which encourages disintegration. Similarly, there is a structuring of the minds of a team that can formulate the multiple problems of the borderline patient, contain countertransference responses, and minimize enactment, thereby improving integration. This allows the development of a capacity to mentalize, stimulates the formation of an increasingly secure attachment, redirects aggression, and improves affect regulation. Day hospital seems a promising alternative to inpatient treatment. Whether it is better than intensive out-patient psychoanalytic treatment for severe BPD remains to be seen.

CHAPTER FOUR

On the therapist's reverie and containing function

Grigoris Vaslamatzis

N ew ideas in psychoanalytic theory and technique always stem from older contributions. Klein, introducing her concept of projective identification, re-estimated Freud's formulations on early object relationships. Klein considered that the internal mental mechanisms (e.g. projection) and drives imprint their action on unconscious phantasies (like projection identification). In her text "Notes on Some Schizoid Mechanisms" (Klein, 1946), she makes reference to the outbursts of anger in infants and records that "the other line of attack derives from the anal and urethral impulses and implies expelling dangerous substances (excrement) out of the self and into the mother. Together with these harmful excrements expelled in hatred, split-off parts of the ego are also projected into the mother . . . are meant not only to injure the object but also to control it and take possession of it" (p. 102).

The original version of this chapter appeared in *Psychoanalytic Quarterly*, 68 (1999, No. 3): 431–440; reproduced by permission.

Bion, continuing this line of thought, has transposed this from what happens to an infant into what happens in the link between mother and infant. He gave emphasis to the mother's ability to contain the primitive anxieties that the infant experiences and that are projected into her.

This description of link is facilitated by a bipolar image: the metaphor of the container and the contained. As such, Bion refers to the very early relationship of the infant to its mother's breast—that is, when the infant directs its anxieties onto the breast. If this experience is pleasant (a mother who can endure and contain anxiety), a feeling of reassurance is established. If the experience is not pleasant (a mother who is anxious and unable to hold the aggressive and anxious trends of her infant), then the response sent does not contain any processing of the projected material, which in turn inundates its immature ego. As Elisabeth Bianchedi (see Vergopoulo, 1996) has pointed out, the mother's mind functions as a link, and in this sense the breast is a link (p. 575).

Although Winnicott was the first to place the creation of the subject in the space between the infant and mother, it was Bion who described an important new concept in psychoanalysis: namely, the links between human beings. He described L (Love), H (Hate), and K (Knowledge), and their counterparts –L, –H, –K, in order to bring together cognition and emotion and to determine the patterns of relationships between infant and parent connected to growth and psychic equilibrium.

In this relationship, Bion includes another aspect: the mother's reverie, which complements the infant's projective phantasies. Reverie is a specific function of the mother which allows her to feel the infant in her, and to give shape and words to the infant's experience. This, according to Bion, is possible since the mother is influenced by the infant's preverbal material (i.e. she is influenced by his projective identifications) and produces her own thoughts and reveries, in which this given material is processed in her own particular way (Bion, 1959, 1962).

The clinical value of the container–contained and reverie concepts is underlined by another analyst, Ogden. His conceptualizations could be seen as a contribution to the better understanding of the transference–countertransference interaction. According to Ogden (1994), during a session

> the analyst's psychological life in the consulting-room with the patient takes the form of reverie, concerning the ordinary, everyday details of his own life ... which are not simply reflections of inattentiveness, narcissistic self-involvement, and the like ... rather it represents symbolic and protosymbolic (sensation-based) forms given to the unarticulated (and often not yet felt) experience of the analysand ... [p. 82]

This psychological activity is often viewed as a disturbing experience by the analyst, who then tries to deny or overcome it—that is to say, to be emotionally present with the patient. Ogden not only acknowledged reverie but he embodied it in his analysis of the transference–countertransference phenomena. Moreover, he proposed a new conceptualization of the analytic process by his notion of the analytic third. He writes: "The analytic third, this third subjectivity is a product of a unique dialectic generated by/between the separate subjectivities of an analyst and analysand within the analytic setting" (p. 64).

In this respect, reverie is a unique experience of the therapist and is connected with countertransference. The elucidation and the in-depth analysis of these experiences will allow, progressively during the therapy, reverie to become a useful therapeutic function along with understanding and interpretation. In conceptualizing reveries, Ogden (1997) stressed that they are derived from the "interplay of the unconscious life of the analysand and that of the analyst" (p. 593) and that the creation of reveries is partly an unconscious intersubjective construction (p. 569).

The analysis of preverbal experience is a prerequisite for an analyst who is sensitive to non-verbal communication and countertransference and who simultaneously endeavours to put into words and describe non-verbally expressed anxieties. The analyst might take into consideration that he or she must become the container of the non-verbally expressed anxieties and subsequently must then understand them with empathy, as the patient has the need to project these anxieties and the unbearable aspects of his or her personality, being unable to endure them or expecting someone else to understand what he or she has experienced. In this process, moreover, containment and interpretation coexist and are viewed in an overall analytic relationship. It is evident that a successful process will be formed when the therapist discovers the specific method of function for his or her patient: when to speak, when to interpret, and when to be silent.

Clinical vignettes

To clarify these theoretical points, I present some clinical fragments from two analytic therapies.

Ms X

The first case refers to a patient whose major difficulties were centred on sadomasochistic enactments in her close relationships. During the third year of her analysis, Ms X started to feel that my interventions and the insight she was achieving during the session caused her pain. Subsequently, I also realized that I was being very cautious, so that re-enactments of her traumas would not be reported in the process of the analysis. I supposed that at this time period, in which the process of understanding within the analytic relationship had stopped, the key link was –K.

In a Friday session, Ms X appeared uninterested and detached; she remained silent for a long time. I noticed that the position of her body was different from that of other times. Her hands were placed in such a way that her face was hidden from my view. She sat much deeper in the couch, and her stance revealed that she was distant. Although the overall picture depicted a state of calmness, it became apparent to me that she was trying to hide something of herself.

Later, when Ms X was still silent, I began to have a reverie. An incident came to mind that had happened with one of my colleagues at a seminar two or three days before and had affected me negatively. I had felt annoyed with this colleague for the way in which she had spoken about one of her patients. I also recalled the anger I had felt, as well as my derogatory thoughts. This, in turn, brought to mind a similar incident many years ago with another colleague. These recollections startled me, and I wondered why they had surfaced now. I could not even understand whether this had something to do with my patient.

As Ms X spoke, I concentrated again on her associations. She made reference to another woman at work whom Ms X disliked intensely, and she felt that the other woman reciprocated the same feelings. Ms X complained about the unethical way her colleague worked. I realized that this woman was being presented as a totally bad person. Then, she said, the thought that this woman might be a patient of mine had crossed her mind and made her furious. The anger was directed towards both her colleague and me. Her associations were accompanied, for the first time at this period of detachment and stalemate, by emotions of anger and disappointment and had created an uneasy atmosphere. Consequently, Ms X had mentioned that this thought now seemed to her as paranoid and she could not understand what had caused her to think of such a thing. She asked me to help her to find the meaning of these feelings. Ms X then relaxed. Her posture changed, and she became thoughtful. My mind, too, became clearer, and the session proceeded on the issue of her anger.

Following Bion's formulations, we can see this communication as a mixture of links in –K and in H, and then a K link is present again.

Focusing now on my reverie, I observed that, in this theme, on two occasions there was a figure towards which my anger was directed. It was an unexpected entrance into my consciousness of a theme of my own personal life—that is, a bad object: the negative feelings towards my colleagues, the feelings of annoyance connected with these thoughts, and finally the effort to accept and tolerate these feelings. But if the reverie was an independent quality of the container, then we have to consider container and contained as a linear process and not as a complex communication, which was Bion's intention. Analysing the reverie of the mother/therapist, the influences from the infant/patient should also be included. Moreover, the container–contained relationship stresses the reciprocity axiom: reverie is the product both of the mother (or therapist) and of the infant (or patient). Following these theoretical notes, we have to broaden the analysis of the clinical instance: the patient, Ms X, could not bear to contain the bad object (of her childhood) in her mind and to elaborate and transform her bad feelings. Perhaps this was due to her incapacity to function as a container of them. She tried to escape from the pain by hiding herself. The therapist had these reveries as a resonance of Ms X's inner struggle with these emotions. He was now the person who contains and who suffers (annoyance, wondering); he was the container of her projections. At the same time, an elaboration of these projections in his psyche, in his internal object relations, was happening. When Ms X started to speak—not only after her silence but also after her therapist's silence, which was filled by his angry feelings—she gave the verbal form of the persecutory anxieties attributable to a very close person. All the intensity of her feelings and the psychic pain was contained in the first instance in the context of non-verbal communication; then, they were contained in the verbal communication.

I would like to add, following Bion's and Ogden's ideas, that not only was a complex communication revealed in the session, but, beyond that, a transition of the patient's experiences—through the reverie of the therapist—had happened. This fact makes the contained more tolerable and enables the persecutory anxieties and the anger to be discussed, as the last part of the session showed. She came back to the process of thinking because her anxieties and feelings were contained in the therapeutic dyad.

Ms L

The second case is Ms L, a patient who some years ago had come for therapy, one year after her father's death, when she felt that she was at deadlock with all her relationships. A decade previously she had had her first analysis, which she interrupted after three years. With regard to this experience, she had declared that "the analysis and my therapist had provided me with absolutely nothing". She could not remember anything from her treatment, and if she were to meet her therapist again she would not even recognize her.

In the course of therapy, it became apparent that a central issue was the effort of Ms L to become relieved from her excessive and prolonged mourning, and more precisely from her internal dead object. I made the conjecture that using projective identifications she was led to relationships characterized by feelings of misery, dissatisfaction, and death on both sides. This was understood as the repetition of her past. For several reasons, which gradually appeared in her associations, her parents decathected from little L, and an unresolved dead-mother complex was formed. We owe the description of this complex to André Green (1986). According to him, the basic characteristics in this case are, first, that it takes place *in* the presence of the object, which is itself absorbed by a bereavement, and, second, that the loss in this case is "the loss of meaning".

During the first year of her present analytic therapy, a similar situation appeared in the therapeutic relationship. The aim of the projective identifications of Ms L—who at the time was filled with despair, depression, and thoughts of suicide—was that the therapist should contain the dead object and the despair. This had been manifested in a session when I realized, for no reason, that I was in an unpleasant and tense state of mind. Feeling sad, I was unable to find any words to help her; my mind went blank. Then I questioned the possibility of changing the therapeutic setting to that of a supportive technique or to that of giving her medication, as she herself had also asked for it. While I was thinking about this, I went into a reverie about my own children. I was trying to imagine what they would ask of me when I returned home. Then I was brought back to my patient, and I thought that a good parent should be a good therapist. I was not sure if this thought was mine or whether I had heard it. Then I felt better and more secure. Once more I was able to discuss the origins of her emotions and her difficulties in her relationships. The session continued in a smoother way, although Ms L kept complaining about her life's miseries. Leaving my office, I tried to understand why I "escaped" from my patient by thinking about the alteration of the setting and by sinking into a reverie about my own family. Because this session was distressing for me, I could not reach a conclusion; but I wondered whether my reverie was related to Ms L's pressure on me to contain her and care for her as an infant.

Coming to the next session, she immediately said that after our previous session "her burden had diminished, since she was able to speak and was released", because perhaps she "felt free and could communicate with her therapist, without theories interfering". Later on, she referred to a dream in which *she was in her therapy hour, the climate had taken an erotic turn, and the therapist had told her that there was a reason for terminating it, and she had said "that is why I was sad". Then the therapist stood up and disappeared, jumping out of the window. Feeling terrified, she ran to see what had happened and saw that her therapist had got up and was fine, having sustained only a few cuts on his face.*

This dream represented many different levels of the transference–countertransference interaction. In brief, my understanding is as follows: initially there is a good (erotic) relationship with the object, which finally withdraws and is transformed to a dead object; thereafter, she pursues bringing it back into her life. With regard to the whole situation, due to identification with the internal dead object Ms L was led to think of committing suicide or to have a deep feeling of death. Also, my inability to find the words and my

thoughts to change the setting were in part due to my identification with the projected-into-me dead object. At the same
time, it was an opportunity for her to have these projections
elaborated so as to make the psychic pain more tolerable and
to ensure a reparation process. I hypothesize that my capacity for reverie, in parallel with the avoidance of acting in any
way, permitted an elaboration of the patient's painful feelings, but in the form of the painful feelings I myself felt, not
unlike a "sojourn" (Bion, 1967, p. 92).

Conclusion

Grotstein (1981), discussing the nature of projective identification, clarified that reverie refers to (maternal) receptivity, including the mother's mental activity when the infant normally
projects into her. In a footnote he adds:

> In psychoanalytic practice, the analyst uses a reverie, corre-
> sponding to Bion's maternal reverie, which allows for the
> *entrance* of the projective identifications as countertransfer-
> ence or as projective counter-identifications, which can then
> be prismatically sorted out and lent themselves to effective
> understanding and ultimately to interpretations. [p. 134]

According to this statement, therapists should allow the entrance of the projections of their patients into their mind. Reverie is an indicator of their receptivity. It is also a function of the
therapists' mind to elaborate, give shape and meaning, and finally communicate verbally something that patients are not yet
able to transform into the verbal or deny it as being painful.
Disavowed parts of the personality could find a way to be understood and to be better contained. [The difficulties lie in
clearly describing and analysing what intersubjective unconscious communication is and how it occurs. Bion (1962) uses
maternal reveries as a metaphor because he perceives them as
an indication that there are links with the child. At the clinical
level, Grinberg (1990) suggests a transformation in the analyst's

personality, a state of convergence with the anxieties and emotions experienced by the patient. Analyst's reveries should emerge as a response to unconscious communication from the patient (Jacobs, 1993, p. 7). It is true that Jacobs avoids using the Bionian terminology such as reverie: he prefers to refer to the "subjective experiences of the analyst" and to his "unconnected memories" as a reflection of both the patient's communications and influences and the analyst's capacity to empathize with the psychic pain of the analysand.]

This might be a new direction, a risk of the psychoanalytic technique which could be successful or not, but at least should permit therapists to encompass their whole personality for the benefit of their patients.

CHAPTER FIVE

Psychodynamic therapy of severe personality disorders

Peter Hartocollis

In specifying the patient population of my treatment approach as "severe personality disorders", I mean to differentiate that group which Otto Kernberg (1975) has designated as "borderline"—that is, patients with a "low-level" character disorder, such as infantile or pseudo-hysterical, paranoid, schizoaffective, and pre-psychotic personality disorders—from "high-level" character disorders of a more benign pathology, such as the hysterical, the obsessive, the depressive, and many, but by no means all, narcissistic personality disorders. In defining my patients in such a way, I mean to imply two things: first, that "higher-level" character disorders are treatable with classical or modified psychoanalysis; second, that the existence of borderline features in many personality disorders does not justify their inclusion under the diagnostic category of "borderline patients", as European colleagues appear to have a tendency to do. In making the diagnosis of a borderline personality disorder, I follow a scheme that has reference to five intertwined areas of psychological function: personal identity, affective lability (and, by extension, impulse control), defensive configuration, reality testing, and interpersonal relations (Hartocollis, 1987). Pathological manifestations in one area have repercussions in any and all other areas, a fact that determines whether or not patients may be treated psychotherapeutically without hospitalization or medication, as when they become suicidal or acutely psychotic.

In doing psychotherapy with patients who manifest a severe personality disorder, I follow psychoanalytic clinical theory, being hardly concerned with psychoanalytic metapsychology. In other words, I am guided by Freud's insights about transference and interpretation, without looking for causative factors like infantile traumata or pseudo-explanatory concepts like unconscious fantasies, infantile conflicts, dammed-up energy because of repressed libidinal or aggressive drives, or dangerous excitation behind which hides a putative death instinct. I am concerned with unconscious object relations only as paradigmatic models of dealing with interpersonal relations, keeping always in focus the transferential, here-and-now communication between patients and myself in the therapeutic situation. Within the boundaries of this transferential, real, and actual but not realistic therapeutic relationship, I demonstrate to patients the pathology of their psychic mechanisms or defences, with which they try to manage the pressure of their wishes, encoded in erotic aggressive and self-destructive fantasies and in affects deriving from a very bad, aggressive, and self-destructive world of internal object relations amounting to a bad, perverted, hateful, angry, and undervalued self-image.

To demonstrate to patients their pathology, starting from the irascible, maladaptive mode of their behaviour and affects, I mainly employ confrontation, through which I pass into the interpretation of their attitude towards the therapist and the meaning of this attitude in the analytic relationship by pointing to the patients' unconscious, behind which, presumably, hide forbidden, conflictual wishes that reflect the state of their primitive internal world of objects and their own problematic—and painfully unacceptable to their self-image. In the process, I point to the patients' primitive defence mechanisms such as splitting, denial, projective identification, psychotic ideas of omnipotence as well as unstable, pseudo-neurotic, and often hypochondrical or psychosomatic symptoms, which weaken their ego strength rather than helping them stand up against their fears and achieve their unconscious intentions, pleasurable wishes, and creative ambitions.

As for the attitude of patients towards the therapist, which is typically underlined by the affects of anger, envy, entitlement, disgust, boredom, emptiness, and anaclitic depression, I see it as motivated primarily by the mental mechanism of splitting. The internal object world of the patients, being composed of contradictory self- and object images cathected by contradictory wishes or intentions, makes them view the therapist alternately either as an exclusively good object or as an exclusively bad object. Splitting the object into good and bad, accompanied by intense, anxiety-ridden ambivalence, corresponds to a splitting of the wish (intention or purpose) into an attitude of approach or withdrawal concerning the therapist. Such an oscillation in the attitude of the patients from that of approach to that of withdrawal, and vice versa, creates in the therapist, contertrans-ferentially, the impression of provocation. When the therapist is viewed exclusively as a good object, patients are experienced as oscillating in their attitude according to a wish or intention for closeness or a defensive counter-wish for distancing themselves from the therapist, a bipolar oscillation that is manifested alternately as admiration or contempt; love or hate; disclosing, confessional behaviour or secretive, lying behaviour; seductive behaviour or repulsive behaviour; receptive, accepting behaviour or rejecting, denouncing behaviour; seeking, full of interest behaviour or indifferent, alienated behaviour. When the therapist is viewed exclusively as a bad object, patients are experienced as oscillating between excitement and boredom; as insulting or pleasing; as scared or reassured; as destructive or protective; as giving or defensive; as confused (mad) or clear-minded and insightful.

Guided by his or her empathic understanding, the therapist perceives the attitude of patients towards him or her in terms of its intentionality, which is unconsciously motivated by the wish to control him or her, inducing the therapist into a particular attitude and eventually behaviour complementary to the patients' own attitude. This hidden intentionality on the part of patients—recognized already by Frieda Fromm-Reichmann (1955) and implied in discussions on the subject of empathy that had been going on long before the concept became Kohut's (1959) and his self-psychology's therapeutic trademark—is the motivating factor behind the phenomenon of enactment that has become the centre of attention of the contemporary movement of intersubjective psychoanalysis.

Concerning empathy, a concept originating in aesthetics, Freud (1914b), in discussing Michelangelo's statue of Moses, wrote: "what grips us so powerfully can only be the artist's *intention*" (p. 212; emphasis in original). It is the intention of patients in the therapeutic relationship to elicit an effect in the therapist. One such effect would be making the therapist understand how patients feel and how they view things—which invariably means to have the analyst agree with the patients and the way they feel or how they view things. Another would be making the therapist love them—which, as Karl Menninger (1988) has shown, has implications of "praise, acceptance, approval, forgiveness, sympathy, audience, help, relief, cure", and—in a deeper, psychodynamic sense—gifts of love, like "greater strength, beauty, power, a penis (or a larger penis), a baby [. . .], according to the specific needs, real or imagined, of the patient either in a past situation or in his present reality situation" (p. 67).

The therapist's empathic understanding of the patients' intention in the therapeutic relationship—which is hardly therapeutic from the patients' point of view—allows the therapist to reveal the patients' secret infantile needs and conflictual, ambivalent wishes concerning the therapist. Confronting them with their aggressive, self-destructive potential and interpreting their negative transference enhances the patients' ego strength and prevents premature termination of treatment—a constant threat because of the patients' readiness for acting-out. Empathic understanding could be often perceived by patients as fulfilment of their wishes, actualizing their transference fantasies by assuming Winnicott's (1960) "holding function" or Kohut's (1971) position in the so-called mirror transference.

Both Kohut (1959) and Kernberg (1975) stress the importance of empathy in the comprehension and treatment of severe personality disorders. Even though in the *Standard Edition* the term *Einfühlung*—"empathy"—never appears "in a clinical sense" (Pigman, 1995, p. 237), Freud (1921c, p. 110, n. 2) did say that empathy is indispensable for the understanding of another person's mental life. In fact, his daring reconstructions in the Dora case—and, I might say, in the Wolf Man and Rat Man cases as well—could be made only by means of empathy. Despite the therapist's best intentions, failures in empathic understanding as well as mistakes in interpretation derived from theoretical bias occur frequently enough in the long run. Sometimes the failure may be only in the patients' mind, if it happens to trigger a negative transference reaction, as when the therapist's intervention evokes in patients a similar parental response in their childhood which was experienced as unempathic. Empathic failures with neurotic patients may be overcome rather easily, whereas in the therapy of severe personality disorders these could be quite destructive.

Psychoanalysts have always stressed the importance of the wish (or desire, according to French colleagues) in the neurotic fantasies of patients—the forbidden, conflictual wish in particular. A wish, however, is different from an intention in that the latter involves action, an attempt to make the wish come true by employing a certain mode of behaviour or thinking, which in psychotherapy manifests itself in the attitude of the patients and in the way they express themselves verbally, both of which make for the phenomenon of enactment (Johan, 1992). In the psychotherapy of borderline patients, this enactment is experienced by the therapist as provocation, which, as I mentioned earlier, oscillates according to the way in which the therapist is perceived in the transference: when the therapist is perceived as a good object, the provocation assumes the character of seduction, the patients' intention being to seduce or to be seduced by the therapist; alternatively, when the therapist is perceived as a bad object, the provocation takes the character of rejection, the patients' intention being to distance themselves from the therapist by either moving away or destroying the relationship. The therapist may respond countertransferentially with his or her own enactment, an unconscious reaction that manifests itself in his or her interventions during therapy—mainly by the therapist's confrontations, which the patients are in all likelihood going to experience as provocative, or by his or her interpretations, which the patients are in all likelihood going to experience as manipulative.

Besides the mechanism of splitting, which conditions borderline patients' intentions, a major carrier of enactment is projective identification. Based on their unconscious intention to relieve themselves from some bad aspect of their self-image, the patients projectively identify it with the therapist, who may be induced to respond in kind. In such a case we have what is known as the "actualization of transference" (Roughton, 1993), which occurs when the patients experience the analyst's attitude or behaviour as having fulfilled their wishes, often without awareness of the wish or the intention.

CHAPTER SIX

Self-envy and intrapsychic interpretation in borderline states

Rafael E. Lopez-Corvo

I n 1949, the Existential psychiatrist Ludwig Biswanger conceived of man as immersed in three different kinds of interacting worlds: *Umwelt*, or environmental; *Mitwelt*, defining his continuous relation with his fellow men; and *Eigenwelt*, representing each person's own inner and intimate world. "Classical psychoanalysis", said Biswanger (1947) "has only a shadowy, epi-phenomenal concept of *Mitwelt* and no real concept of *Eigenwelt*." If I were to extrapolate these notions and compare them with the different forms of interpretation as they are known today, *Umwelt* and *Mitwelt* could correspond to extra-transference and transference interpretations, respectively. *Eigenwelt* seems to be left out of this picture, as if Biswanger's assumption were still appropriate and interaction of inner elements within the self were not yet provided with a necessary

The original version of this chapter appeared in *Psychoanalytic Quarterly*, 68 (1999, No. 2): 209–219; reproduced by permission.

relevance—perhaps with the exception of Paula Heimann's (1952) contribution on paranoid states.

At least from a theoretical point of view, if the aim of extra-transference interpretation is to move towards transference, the purpose of transference interpretation would then be intrapsychic, because transference is not the real fact, the final truth: it is a fatalistic complication of derivative continuous repetition. On the other hand, intrapsychic interpretation—of the interaction of part and total self-object representations—would be the end of the quest. Introjection of projected objects (Freud, 1921c) and resolution of transference are important signals to be taken into account once termination of analysis has been considered.

Self-envy

The importance of intrapsychic interpretation became obvious to me while researching the dynamic of "self-envy" in border-line structures, and this has led me to attempt a brief description of self-envy at this time. The condition of self-envy results from the interaction of different elements that conform to the Oedipus complex (Lopez-Corvo, 1992, 1994). There are cases where a child who has felt excluded experiences an increment of envy during childhood towards the parental couple—for example, envy of such aspects as parental harmony, power, control, creativity, capacity to reproduce, and so on. Those envious feelings experienced by the child towards his or her parents will remain inside as foreign and active objects, without being assimilated within the ego (Heimann, 1952). When children like this grow and become adults themselves, they will then envy in themselves their own capacity to have a harmonious relationship, to create, to exercise control, and so forth just as they envied their own parents in the past. I believe that self-envy is a more common dynamic than we have thought.

Gregory

"Gregory", 24 years old, and the elder of two brothers, had been in analysis for the past three years because of depressive bouts and other difficulties related to his university studies. There was also great envy of and rivalry with his younger brother, who, Gregory feels, was favoured by his parents and, according to him, was just the opposite of himself: easygoing, with a lot of friends, and very successful with women. However, it was pointed out to Gregory what a poor academic achiever his brother was, in comparison with his own successful university accomplishments. Lately Gregory has been working at a hospital while writing his thesis, and he expects to graduate six months from now. Also, different from before, he has been missing sessions and is one month behind in his payments. He explained that lately he felt rather confused, not functioning properly or working well on his thesis or in his job at the hospital and attending poorly at the university. It became clear that his graduation was causing a great deal of anxiety at that particular moment, inducing intense feelings of unconscious envy against the "graduating aspect" of himself, understood as a subtle but continuous attempt to undermine his desire to achieve it. And this is exactly what I pointed out to him: his own inner difficulty between one aspect that wished to succeed and another that continuously and simultaneously spoiled it.

During the previous session, Gregory had talked about joining a volleyball team at the university, and as usual he feared that he could unconsciously sabotage the games and make the team lose. He remembered when he was in primary school and there had been a writing and spelling contest. Because he knew more English than the other students, he was asked to be the last one to compete. However, when his turn came, "I made the stupidest mistake you could think of and my team, which was ahead, lost". He continued, explaining that he has always been afraid of winning. Then I told him that he envied winners so much that he has to make sure that he was not one of them.

At the next session, the last in November, he handed over a cheque with the payment for the month of October, already long overdue. I made the comment that November was not included. He answered that lately he was very confused and that he was not doing anything right, and he continued with the intention of repeating the same previous pattern of punishing himself before he was punished. After a silence, he remembered a dream:

He was driving his car at night, but his vision was significantly blurred. Suddenly, he hit a man who was cutting the grass at one side of the road. There was blood all over the car, which was badly dented. A lot of people started to walk towards him saying: "Now you are really in trouble—look what you have done. You cannot continue driving if you cannot see right." But he continued driving, and further on he hit a woman on the pavement who was holding a child, killing them both and repeating the previous gory scene. As before, people approached him insisting that he should not continue driving, but he persisted and the situation was repeated perhaps once again. He woke up sweating, very anxious, and feeling very pleased that it was just a dream.

After a short silence and giving no associations, I said that there were three main elements in the dream: a blind killer, several victims, and an accusing chorus. He added that it was like a Greek tragedy, like Antigone or some other tragedy, where the chorus was always pointing out the truth. This "killer" aspect was attacking the working part in himself, as well as the possibility of becoming—after graduating—his mother's favoured child (the woman with a child), attacking as well my "working patient" by missing sessions and the analyst also by not paying on time. "Blind" with envy, an excluded part-object now introjected was, as part of his inner drama within the self, destroying idealized aspects—of himself and of the others—that were also introjected objects.

Transference collusion
and superego projections

There are at least two other situations besides the dynamic of self-envy where intrapsychic interpretation could be very useful. I am thinking, in the first place, about the danger of a transference collusion in patients suffering from important perverse or paranoid psychopathology; in the second, those cases where there is a possibility of projections of superego aspects into the analyst and, as a consequence, the danger of the patient experiencing most of the interpretations as accusations.

Transference collusion

Let us now see a case where intrapsychic interpretation is preferred in order to avoid a perverse homosexual collusion from a patient who originally complained of difficulties with penile erection.

Lately we have observed a certain tendency in "Ray"—a 26-year-old in his second year of analysis—to repeat my interpretations, pursuing further whatever I might have expressed, adding to my hypothesis other interests of his own, or corroborating what I might have said. At one point, I had the impression that we were two analysts discussing the case of a patient who was not there. Afterwards, this changed into a tendency to complain continuously about not being able to accomplish what his parents expected of him— not to work while studying, not to have friends or to date girls. His unfair accusations induced the countertransference feeling that he, like his parents, was also complaining that I was not helping him to achieve these goals. The unfairness of this demand also induced a desire to defend myself, and I recognized in the countertransference the presence of a certain anger, also acted out by him whenever he decided not to do what he felt his parents wanted. As I interpreted these

62   RAFAEL E. LOPEZ-CORVO

aspects, he started to remain silent for several minutes at the beginning of each session, complaining that he found it difficult to say exactly what he was thinking. The session I am now presenting was the first one after the Easter holiday. As usual, he remained silent for the first ten minutes; then he said:

Ray: "I always feel that I remain silent and that I waste my time. Sometimes I think before I come here about some things that I consider very important, and I say: I will say this to the doctor. But then I arrive here and I remain silent and say nothing, and I start to think about other things, many things that go through my mind very rapidly, and whatever I was thinking before I don't think about any more, and then I say nothing, I become mute. And I remember what you once said—that I was preparing the sessions."

A: (*I wish to interpret his resistance, his dissociation*) "It seems as if there is one Ray that wishes to hide another Ray."

Ray: "Well, I feel as if there is a part of me that is only mine, something very intimate, that it is only my own business. And I think: how could it be of any importance to the doctor if I tell him that the battery of my car is discharged because I didn't use my car during the holidays, and that I have to recharge it, or that I have to go to the supermarket to get food because my parents are not here now?"

A: (*I think that I have to insist on overcoming the resistance, the dissociation, but also to help him to see that what he is leaving out is perhaps very important*) "Perhaps you fear to let yourself know that I could be very important for you and that you might need me, that while I was away you felt discharged and empty, and that now you are coming back here to recharge yourself again. Perhaps you also feel angry because you had to feed yourself alone."

Ray: (*Silent for a few minutes*) "In the religious books like the

Torah, the rabbi searches for all sorts of words in order to find all kinds of meanings. For instance, if such a word is repeated several times in a paragraph, that would mean that a war against Iraq was going to take place in 1990, as if something that was said so many years ago could have something to do with the present time, as if they already knew what was going to happen. And if I were to ask, 'Well, Rabbi, prove it to me that what you are saying is true', I feel that it would be an impudence, that I would be disrespectful of him. Here I feel the same way—that when you say that the battery is discharged, I wonder what in the heck has this to do with me. I feel like saying also, 'Well Doctor, prove it to me', but I feel that it will be, like, disrespectful of you also."

A: (*I feel the power of a projective identification, the danger of a transference collusion, that he wishes to get involved in a discussion with me as a homosexual resistance in order to protect himself from the anxiety induced by his ambivalence from a homosexual need to be possessed, the presence of a needy, helpless, and envious element that feels that whatever the Other might have to say is the absolute truth. I feel at this moment that the best strategy would be to show the conflict between the parts, to provide an intrapsychic interpretation*) "It seems as if you feel trapped between a Ray that needs so much to please and to feel wanted, and this need makes you feel very angry, as if you have no will power, and another hidden Ray that you fear to let go of, to share, and who questions everything, regardless if it is important for you or not."

Ray: "The problem is that I always accept whatever the others say, my father, the rabbi, you. And you are right, there is this little me inside, that whenever you, or my father, or the rabbi says something, this little me says, 'Why should I accept anything.' But then I feel frightened, I feel as if I am bad, that I am bad if I said something against it or if I question it."

Superego projections

Finally, there is the use of intrapsychic interpretation for the purpose of dealing with superego projections, which usually induce persecution and guilt in patients with important melancholic features.

Amelia

"Amelia" is a 28-year-old housewife, in analysis for the past eight months, who consulted because of marital problems in her second marriage. She is the eldest of four sisters, and there was a history of resentment and sibling rivalry because she felt she always received the worst in her family. From a very early age Amelia was considered a "problem child", and she was seen by a school psychologist around her fourth grade because she was accused of being verbally as well as physically abusive towards other children. Her adolescence was not easy either: she was rebellious, acted out frequently, had poor grades, and, for a while, consumed marijuana. When she was 18 she had to get married because she was pregnant, getting divorced shortly after giving birth to a girl who is now 10 years of age. At the present time she is giving great importance to her decision of going back to the university. She is taking a course in economics and feels very happy about it, "Because it's different from before, now I am studying for myself instead of doing it to please my parents, as I used to do before". Two years ago she married again. Everything was going well, but then they started to have problems, because, as she puts it: "He is too jealous and I am too aggressive. We have too many discussions, and I don't want to get a divorce again." Amelia is an intelligent and very attractive, coquettish, and seductive young woman, always dressing in very short skirts and very low necked dresses, as well as using a generous amount of makeup. There was a dissociation in the transference between her exhibitionism, on the one hand, and a feeling of low self-esteem, on the other, frequently fearing being scolded that she has nothing good to offer or to say, resulting in certain difficulty to free-associate. Countertransferentially, I am aware of her attractiveness, although her exhibitionism does not elicit any erotic feeling. However, I feel that I should be cautious of falling into the temptation of an exhibitionist–voyeuristic couple. I would like now to refer to a session, the first one of her four weekly sessions.

Amelia: "This weekend I had a fight with my husband. Things had improved for a while, perhaps because I am less aggressive than before. This Saturday I was back from the university, where I am taking a course in administration. He was watching TV. He was watching it the whole morning. Lately I try not to say anything about it, but I get very irritated when I see him like that, only watching TV, because he pays no attention to anything— the world could collapse and he wouldn't move. At the beginning, to catch his attention, I used to undress myself in front of the television. All that he does is watch TV and nothing else. Yesterday, I said that he looks like an idiot, with his mouth open and drooling, watching that stupid TV all day. I told him that he was going to become an imbecile, but he didn't answer me and then I threw a mango I was eating and it hit him on the head. He got furious and started to scream at me and then we insulted each other."

There was a pause at this moment, and I decided to interpret; however, I was aware of the danger—of inducing resistances, of increasing the superego sadism, throwing a "mango" at her head, instead of helping her to gain insight— were I to say, for instance, that she felt like a TV herself, that she wanted to compete with television, because what she really wanted was for all of us to drool while watching her, and that she felt very angry when this didn't happen. I decided to interpret in a different form:

A: "Perhaps some anger that you feel against your husband is also against yourself—or, better, against a powerful part inside you that creates for you a real trap and great confusion, not knowing exactly what is more important for you, either "imbecilizing" yourself and changing into a TV, while changing all of us into imbeciles, drooling while watching you, or using your head and your intelligence instead, which you are also trying to educate by bringing to the university. Angry with being trapped, confused for not really knowing what is more important for you, your body or your head."

Amelia was silent for a short while, and then she said: "I have never seen things in this way before."

By interpreting in this manner I was attempting to place the conflict inside, because her anger was not only about her husband preferring the TV instead of herself, but also against herself, because of her need to compete with a television. Placing the conflict between two different parts of her self, I was also avoiding the danger of eliciting further superego sadism by inducing self-accusation, as I would have if I had identified only her unconscious exhibitionistic transferential wish of competing with a television. After all, this not completely true either, because there was ambivalence in her: it was certain that a very important part of her was interested in a voyeuristic–exhibitionistic interaction, but there were other interests in her, too. At the same time, this interpretation attempted to provide the ego with a better perspective of the conflict, meaning that at the end the problem was the consequence of disparate and opposite interests continuously present within the self, trapping the ego between two different possibilities: (1) either the conviction that being a TV and having everybody drooling over herself was the real core of her oedipal need (i.e. triumphing over her mother for her father's complete attention); or (2) discovering other possibilities of obtaining pleasure by focusing her full energy on developing other interests.

CHAPTER SEVEN

Lust for love

Ilany Kogan

In this chapter, I want to focus on the difficulties in the analytic treatment of analysands who, in order to salvage some psychic equilibrium, rely desperately on a pervasive network of defensive operations and transferences.

For the purpose of illustration, I shall use a case study in which the patient's homosexual identity served in her struggle against an inner emotional deadness and self-destructive fantasies, which could eventually lead her to suicide and psychic death. The transference constellation developed in an adversarial fashion, and it culminated in a crisis in which the patient wanted to break the therapeutic alliance by leaving treatment.

Threatened by the possibility that she might express her hatred and aggression towards me through a self-destructive act, I felt that I had to acquiesce in some way. This realization enabled me to bring a change into my interpretations and come up with a "holding interpretation" (Kogan, 1995, 1997), a soothing and supportive intervention. As a result of this, there was a shift in the transference, which enabled the patient to face her conflicting feelings towards me with less fear and which facilitated the continuation of the analytic process.

Deborah

THE FIRST ENCOUNTER — LUST AND FEAR

Before quoting a few fragments from the patient's analysis to illustrate the above theme, I want to introduce her and provide a glimpse into our first meeting.

"Deborah", a 45-year-old woman, married with seven children (ages 7 to 19 years), came to me asking for psychoanalytic help.

The reason she approached me for analysis emerged through the following story. Deborah was a professional woman, the director of a private enterprise. Some years ago she went abroad with her husband and children, where she became interested in sex therapy and took some courses in a professional school. During her stay abroad she went to psychological treatment, which escalated into a sexual affair with her therapist, a woman, who initiated her into lesbian practices.

For Deborah, the bond with her therapist became very strong, affectively and sexually. She felt that through this love, her self-image as well as her body image have greatly improved. When they parted (because Deborah returned home with her family), she experienced separation as tremendously difficult and painful. The relationship with her husband lost whatever affective meaning it had before. Deborah missed her lover and mourned their separation. The idea of leaving her husband and living with her therapist had crossed her mind, but she never thought that it was realistic. She often called her therapist, just to hear her voice on the answering machine. "I needed this to be reassured of her existence", she said.

Last summer, Deborah went abroad to take part in a programme for students on sex therapy. There, she had an affair
with a woman colleague from the group. She again felt ex-
ulted by the love she experienced for this woman. Deborah's
most exciting fantasy in lesbian relationships was not connected to the sexual organs; rather, it was the holding of
hands and kissing with romantic music in the background.
Again, separation from her lover was difficult and caused
her a lot of pain. However, she recently received a letter
from this woman informing her that she had a new woman
friend, who was living with her. Deborah, confused, restless,
and not knowing what to do, decided to come to treatment.

Deborah explained to me why she had looked for a female
analyst: being familiar with the prohibitions of the profession, she was sure that I would not seduce her. She expressed a wish to do everything possible to prevent this
treatment from becoming a love relationship, as had happened with her sex therapist.

I looked at the woman seated opposite me, who was speaking in a monotonous, quiet voice. She was of ordinary
appearance, blond, plump, regular features, and unsophis-
ticatedly dressed. I noticed a certain lack of expression on her
face, a lack of colour and vitality in her demeanour. What
struck me most of all was the gap between her lack of affective expressiveness and her description of the intense feelings that accompanied her lesbian love affairs.

I gathered from her story that, now abandoned by her second lover and trying to fill a void, she hoped to find in
analysis a potential new lover like the one she found in her
first therapy abroad. At the same time, I believed that she
might be terribly afraid of the realization of her erotic
wishes, especially since the fulfilment of her desires was
connected to separation and pain. The conscious fear of her
unconscious desires and wishes towards me was a theme
that accompanied us throughout the entire treatment.

Being aware that a transferential interpretation of her contradictory pursuits would be immature at this stage of analysis, and that it might be experienced by her as accusatory or humiliating, I kept to myself whatever knowledge I had gathered from our first encounter, hoping to deepen it through our future acquaintance.

ANAMNESIS

Deborah was the daughter of Spanish Jews who emigrated before the Second World War to South America, and from there on to Israel. Her parents both came from large families, and each had several brothers and sisters.

Deborah had only one sister, who was six years her junior. She had virtually no recollection of her childhood years. She knew that her mother suffered from depression while pregnant with her, because she had been told this during adulthood. When Deborah was 26 years old, already married with two children, her mother was hospitalized in a psychiatric ward, suffering from psychotic depression. This episode occurred when her sister, then 20 years old, decided to leave home. Deborah thought that this was the reason for her mother's breakdown, since she could not bear to be separated from her younger daughter. Her sister became a professional woman, but never married or built a life of her own.

Deborah described her mother as a very obsessive and ruminative individual, who perceived people and life from the outside. She was impressed by how they looked and what they said, but without any deeper understanding. The mother was never in touch with feelings—neither her own nor those of others. Deborah felt that for her mother she always remained an extension of herself, that she was never recognized by her as a separate individual.

Deborah's mother had a brother who was diagnosed as schizophrenic. Though having a son of his own, he lived with his mother (Deborah's grandmother), who was herself considered an unstable person. A couple of months after the grandmother's death, this uncle committed suicide.

Deborah's father was an important figure in the community abroad and was greatly admired by Deborah. She perceived him as a rational person and tried to identify with him. With time, she realized that her mother dominated him with her fears. She remembered that he was loving and caring towards her in her childhood, but when she grew older she felt abandoned by him.

Deborah met her first boyfriend at the age of 16. They were very attached to each other, both sexually and emotionally. After some time he left her, claiming that she was still immature.

Her husband, who was 15 years her senior, was already a well-known industrialist when they met. It was a flattering connection for Deborah. He was a friend of her parents and highly appreciated by her father. She was glad about the relationship, but not enthusiastic. Before her wedding, she became depressed and had what she called a "nervous breakdown". Then, like now, she felt she missed the expression of his love in words. She saw her husband, who was by now famous and successful, as a workaholic, always busy in "saving humanity". Deborah considered her marriage unsatisfactory. She felt that she searched all her life for an inner figure, somebody to whom she could be really close.

LUST AND THE INNER DEADNESS

After our initial meetings, I accepted Deborah's request for analysis, and we began treatment four times a week, on the couch.

I do not presume to describe here the whole course of analysis. However, I want to refer to our second meeting, through which I became acquainted with her wounded self and her inner deadness, themes that preoccupied us for many months of analytic work.

In the beginning of this meeting, Deborah referred to her going away from our first encounter hurt and humiliated. Apparently, she thought that she had seen a derogatory smile on my face when she insisted upon being sure that because I am an analyst I would not seduce her. My smile reminded her of her mother's critical attitude towards her. When Deborah was a little child, she had been fat, and her mother, who gave marks to everybody, had beeen critical of Deborah's appearance.

In the countertransference, I felt that I had been assigned two consequential roles right from the beginning: coming to analysis, Deborah expected me to be the seductive, incestuous, and abandoning mother; following that, I became the humiliating, critical, and rejecting mother. This realization made me aware of Deborah's complex and painful relationship with her internal maternal object.

I became acquainted, through the first year of analysis, with Deborah's inability to feel and her emotional deadness. I learned this from the way she tried to revive it by looking at people in situations when they expressed feelings. For example, she used to go to the arrival hall in the airport to watch people meeting and embracing each other passionately. She would stand there looking for hours, never getting bored, drinking in thirstily from strangers the expressions of emotions.

This inner deadness infiltrated almost all the emotional spheres of her life, even her motherhood. When her children were little, she felt she could not relate to them. She used to go to playgrounds where mothers watched their children, and she observed the mothers talking to the children. Deborah tried to experience motherly feelings by identifying with and imitating normal mothers. This was not always successful for her .

Deborah claimed that the only two things that succeeded in reviving her inner deadness were giving birth and falling in love. Only these powerful experiences enabled her to feel emotionally alive.

Listening to Deborah describing her plight, I felt like looking into an abyss. A frightening black hole, a deadly wound, opened up in the place where normal human emotions should have been. What was the terrible experience of lack, I asked myself, that dried up the spring of feelings, creating a desert land, an inner emotional deadness, that could not but make her life meaningless? Or was it the inner deadness of the mother that was now part of the daughter's psychic life?

I did not expect to find the answers to these questions so quickly. I hoped that with the continuation of our analytic work, we would be able to understand more.

LUST AND PERSECUTORY FEARS

I want now to explore the issue of Deborah's self-destructive tendency as it was revealed through her associations and fantasies, mainly during the third year of analysis. I shall first refer to a dream from this period.

"In my dream", said Deborah, *"you came up close to me, touched me, and told me something personal about yourself. I looked at you—there was a woman dancing to the rhythm of jazz music. The woman didn't actually look like you, she was darker, had curly hair, another face. She was not somebody whom I knew, but I felt it was you."*

Deborah's associations to the dream revolved around her children. Her two girls, 12 and 15 years old, danced jazz. She felt that it was much more difficult for her to relate to her girls, with their budding femininity, than to her boys. With the boys, she felt she could be much closer. A memory surfaced about her younger daughter, who, when frustrated and angry, seemed to her as if she wanted to jump out of the window to commit suicide.

We first attempted to explore Deborah's wish to get close to me, her longing to be touched by me, as well as the fear that this closeness entailed. Regarding her difficulty to relate to her girls, as well as to me in the transference, we understood that this difficulty not only stemmed from her fear of her erotic wishes, but also from the envy she felt towards my femininity. But where did her self-destructive tendency, which was expressed through the way she perceived her little girls, come from? Was it possible, I asked myself, that the encounter with a female analyst who did not fulfil her erotic wishes provoked so much anger, frustration, and desperation that Deborah, who actually wanted to destroy me, turned the aggression inwards and wanted to kill herself?

Deborah's further associations continued to revolve around death. She described the way her uncle (her mother's schizophrenic brother) committed suicide. When, shortly after his mother's death, no one was there to keep an eye on him, he left the house, put his head into a swamp, and inhaled the dirty water. He suffocated to death in the mud.

I recognized the message that Deborah was conveying to me through her story: I have to protect her against her self-destructive impulses, otherwise she might drown in them. But what could the swamp be for Deborah, I wondered. Was she, indeed, threatened by psychosis, and to what extent were her defences against psychic death effective to prevent it?

The answer to these questions came through the exploration of Deborah's persecutory fears, which were combined with her lust for erotic love. I illustrate this through an episode from the third year of analysis.

During the summer vacation, Deborah worked abroad in a sex therapy clinic run by a woman therapist, well-known in her field. Deborah claimed that the woman liked her a lot.

Being childless and looking for a professional heiress, she even offered to adopt Deborah. In this clinic, women therapists were employed as surrogates, whose role was to help invalids to function sexually. Deborah worked as a surrogate for a while; during this period a secret fantasy, which she didn't understand, occasionally troubled her. Deborah sometimes felt like slashing her wrists. She did not know where this feeling came from. Life seemed to her so very interesting. It was, indeed, a very strange thought.

Through her story, I realized how much Deborah re-enacted her unconscious conflicts and wishes regarding life and death in this kind of work. Functioning as a surrogate, she consciously fulfilled her wishes to repair a damaged, sexually dead person by giving him the ability to make love. This required from her only erotic love, without any emotional involvement, which perfectly suited her. However, in her unconscious fantasy, Deborah was herself the invalid who needed reparation of a vital function—that of giving and receiving love. By being a surrogate, she attempted to re-vivify the dead part in herself, but, as we can see from her suicidal thoughts, she was unsuccessful in her attempt. Working through this episode, we understand that Deborah wanted to kill herself because love-making in a concrete way was very far from satisfying her emotional needs. Giving and receiving love on a concrete level did not make her inner deadness and the meaninglessness of her life disappear.

I pointed out to Deborah that in analysis she was the emotional cripple who needed revivification of her dead inner self. In this role, she asked me to be her emotional surrogate who, by giving her feelings, was supposed to revive in her the ability to love and enable her to feel alive again.

Until now, there were two things that succeeded in revivifying Deborah's inner emotional deadness: giving birth (hence the large number of children), and falling in love with a woman. I now realized that, being older and giving up the idea of having children, Deborah's whole life revolved around the desperate need for a love relationship with another woman. Could Deborah feel emotionally alive in situations that required from her a healthy respect for the reality of life? Could I help her transform her lust for love into a lust for life?

LUST FOR LIFE

I now want to explore the issue of Deborah's struggle for emotions, as shown from an episode taken from the fourth year of analysis.

Deborah described in detail a farewell party, which she attended when she was abroad with her husband, given in honour of a famous actor who suffered from a terminal illness and was on his death-bed. She and her husband had been invited, together with many television people, actors, and friends. The party, given at the actor's request, was a very special occurrence. For seven hours, people spoke to him and about him, each of them receiving a small farewell gift from him. There was a programme on the television in which the actor's doctor stood on the stage for more than an hour, showing everybody slides of the actor's damaged organs and explaining about his illness.

In the transference, I asked Deborah if I was supposed to become the doctor who is publicizing his patient's internal state. Deborah rejected my interpretation with fury. She often expressed irritation and anger whenever I touched upon our relationship. "You are always pushing yourself into things that belong to reality", she said. "This has nothing to do with you." It was true that she wanted fame and recognition, she added; actually, there was a journalist who had recently been asking her for an interview about her successful career, to publish in a local women's magazine. Such a person could bring her fame and advertise her business.

It was clear to me that Deborah saw me in the transference as a potential instrument for exhibiting herself in public. This is why for many years I recoiled writing about this case. Only now, years after the analysis was finished, and after I "dressed her up" with proper disguises, was I able to describe this treatment and the difficulties I encountered in it.

Deborah's reaction brought to my mind what I already knew about her perverse, exhibitionistic needs. I have learned this from her stories about different courses in sex therapy which she took abroad and which she described with gusto. In one of these "experiential" courses, a group of about twenty women sat in a circle with their legs wide open, exploring their vagina in front of each other. In another course, the students were shown about two hundred slides of female genitalia. Deborah claimed that these courses were intended to help the students overcome their inhibitions.

In my countertransference feelings, I was aware that Deborah wished to play a perverse game with me of comparing our genitalia, in order to make sure that she was a woman. Apparently, only by exhibiting herself in public (in the proximity of women) could she feel that her femininity existed at all.

Continuing her story about the actor, Deborah mentioned that she was very impressed by the party, as well as by the actor himself, whose life story became public knowledge at this stage of his life. He came as a child to the United States from Eastern Europe, where his parents had been destroyed by the Nazis. He lived a very creative but unscrupulous life, being sexually promiscuous, mainly with women but also with men, and losing contact with his family, his wife, and his children. There were rumours that he had been seduced by his mother when he was 13 years old, and that throughout his life he behaved in an antisocial way by seducing minors around the same age. Nothing was ever proved against him, but the scandalous story of his life became a newspaper scoop and was then made into a television series.

Deborah expressed her admiration for the actor and for his way of life. She believed that he achieved complete acceptance of his body and derived a lot of pleasure from his sexual life. She also felt that, like him, she looked for powerful life experiences, but unlike him she gave them up because of social conventions.

The actor's story about being seduced in his adolescence by his mother, evoked Deborah's memories of herself as a child being molested first by a man and then by a woman. She remembered that at the age of 9, a man who worked in her parents' house sat near her and stroked her under her skirt. He asked if she liked it; it was a pleasant feeling. In contrast to this incident, the second one, connected to a woman, was completely masked under the cover of love and affection. Only the context in which it was recalled hinted at a sexual exploitation. At the age of 11, she was in a car with an aunt, her father's sister, who was a nurse by profession. Deborah put her head in her aunt's lap, and the aunt stroked her head. She felt she wanted more and more. The same experience was repeated later with her first female lover, her first therapist. Once, performing a Gestalt exercise, the therapist put her to sleep like a baby, by stroking her hair. It was so good that Deborah wanted it to go on for ever and ever. She felt that she had missed out on that kind of physical affection all her life.

These memories facilitated the elaboration of Deborah's oedipal and pre-oedipal longings. Deborah was conscious of her oedipal attraction to her father, which was further transferred to her husband. She remembered that her father gave her love and caring in childhood, but she always felt the tension of the physical attraction between them. She felt how seductive he was towards her when he was singing love songs to her on his guitar. She believed that her love for her husband stemmed from his similarity to her father.

In the transference, I was suddenly put in the role of the admired but rejecting father (husband)-analyst. Close to Remembrance Day, Deborah happened to see my name in a newspaper, mentioned among Israeli researchers who dealt with the topic of the Holocaust. As a result, a question was evoked in her: how important could she be for me if my real interest lay in life-and-death matters, similar to those that had preoccupied her husband or her father in the past?

Deborah believed that her pre-oedipal longings, which were lived out in her lesbian relationships, stemmed from the affective and physical lack of closeness that she experienced with her mother. She was aware of the frustration she had experienced in her childhood, and she saw her mother responsible for that. She felt that her longing to be touched and caressed by a woman was evoked by the special relationship with her aunt.

In the transference, we got in touch with Deborah's anger and rejection of me, as a result of her frustrated longings to be touched in the analytic situation. Deborah vehemently claimed that she was aware of her "real" needs—she longed for a relationship that would combine sexuality and feelings and would make her "whole". Deborah felt that she could have such a relationship only with a woman, the relationship with a man being only partially satisfying.

When I pointed out to Deborah that she probably longed for closeness on an emotional and physical level with me in treatment, she became outraged: again I was pushing our relationship to the foreground, a fact that she found very irritating. What did her dreams and wishes, her anger and frustration, have to do with me at all? She knew very well how barren and intellectual analysis was; she knew I would never fulfil her wishes to be touched and caressed. "Why do I need such an intensive treatment?" she asked. "I am aware of my strong need for a relationship with a woman. This urge bothers me more and more in analysis, it takes a lot of energy from me. I think if I had such a relationship, I wouldn't need the treatment any more. I wouldn't feel the longing and the loss."

At this stage in analysis, Deborah began to "flirt" with the idea of leaving treatment. I tried to show her how aggressive she was towards me and our work. I reminded her that, at the beginning of treatment, in order to avoid another failure she had warned me not to seduce her like her first therapist did. Now she claimed that the treatment was going to fail unless it included a physical relationship, the only way to save her life. It seemed to me, I added, that she wanted to destroy this treatment even before it started.

The confrontation with Deborah's dead and deadening aspects in the transference remained unfruitful. My attempts to help her realize the cruel and depriving way in which she treated me fell on deaf ears. I felt that my interpretations were becoming repetitious, lifeless, and inefficient. I began to wonder if Deborah could ever give up the idea that only the fulfilment of her homosexual wishes would revive her emotional life. If so, was the "holding"—love, care, and understanding—that I gave her in analysis enough to bring life into her emotional deadness and to fight the thanatic forces expressed through her self-destructive tendencies? To what extent was her homosexual solution vital for this purpose?

A particular dream that showed Deborah's fear of feelings towards me in the transference elucidated some things for me:

"I travelled with my husband, one daughter, and the famous actor whose party I attended. I had fantasies about him and I wanted to stay with him alone. It was a difficult situation; half of his body was paralysed because of the treatment he was undergoing. My husband stated that I, too, suffered from a terminal illness. He decided to bury me. The idea was to put me in the grave, so that I would suffocate and not need to undergo this painful treatment. I didn't take my leave from my children, from friends. I didn't choke, I got up and continued living."

In her associations, Deborah mentioned that the actor's treatment was not only unsuccessful, but also caused him damage. She, like the actor in her dream, came to analysis half numb (emotionally). But what if analysis could injure her more than it could help? She felt that since her emotional illness was fatal, she had to undergo a very painful treatment in order to recover. But, at the same time, she was afraid that the very treatment that was supposed to be life-giving, by evoking her emotions, could be painful to the point that it was life-threatening. Deborah felt that she would rather be numb, paralysed, choking, than be confronted with her feelings towards me. On the other hand, she wanted to get out of the grave, from her inner emotional deadness, in order to feel alive.

What could I do to bring Deborah to life, I asked myself. Being trapped between her aggressive behaviour towards me and her destructiveness towards herself, I felt paralysed. It then occurred to me that the actor, who suffered from paralysis of half of his body, could also represent me and my impotence in helping her realize her hostile aspects. And if this was so, how was I going to get out of the place where I was being suffocated by her rejection and hatred on the one hand, and by my fears for her physical and psychic survival on the other?

Since neither the interpretations of her libidinal needs and wishes, nor those of her aggression or hostility towards me, were ever accepted by Deborah, I felt that I had to find a different way to reach her. I knew that I had to show Deborah that I cared, without ever mentioning my separate existence. I had to recognize her needs and wishes, without linking them directly to me. Finally, I had to touch her positive feelings through my words, so that she would be able to face both her love and her hatred towards me with less shame and humiliation.

A beautiful verse by Rainer Maria Rilke came to my mind and I said: "You shouldn't turn away from treatment. Love consists in this, that two solitudes protect and touch and greet each other."

For some moments we were both silent, and then I saw tears in Deborah's eyes. "I never knew that you really cared about me", she said. Then, she added: "It was always hard for me to have an emotional experience without turning it into something sexual. Feelings seemed so frightening that I needed sex to make it bearable. I wanted you to touch me, to caress me, but deep down I did not want to have any feelings towards you."

This awareness was a breakthrough to Deborah's hate and a change in her transference relation to me. In the subsequent period, Deborah no longer wanted to leave treatment. She no longer asked for further gratification in the form of touching. We were able to work through her demands for physical closeness and attempted to understand their conflicting meaning. For Deborah, touching, though in itself an erotic act and a token of my love, was in the service of Thanatos. Deborah understood that, since feelings threatened her precarious sanity, touching was a way of avoiding feelings and thus keeping on safe but barren ground. She realized that by using touching to survive psychic death, she also kept her emotional deadness intact.

It was only now that we could understand her emphatic demand for an unacceptable course of action as her need to repeat in treatment her childhood trauma, by turning me into the sexual exploiter.

During this period, Deborah had many dreams that showed her heterosexual attraction to men.

A meaningful change occurred when, during the last year of analysis (the fifth), Deborah acquired a new woman friend, Eve. This friendship, though very intimate, never became sexual. Deborah had fantasies about what could become a "real relationship" between them, but she refrained from bringing in sexuality. For the first time when falling in love with a woman, Deborah thought that sex might spoil the relationship and closeness. Through Eve, Deborah expressed how grateful she was to me in analysis: "I do not need to get an orgasm, for this I have a vibrator. Eve is alive, she is a person full of emotions. I was alive on many different levels, but on a deeper level I needed Eve, or you here in treatment, in order to feel alive."

In spite of her still-existing problems—her attraction to women and her inability to feel completely happy in the relationship with her husband—we were both aware of a change in Deborah's attitude to life. She gave up her frantic search for a homosexual partner, not believing any more that this would solve all her problems. A kind of accommodation or compromise solution was reached in regard to her family: she could live with them with more satisfaction. She could also have mutual (not necessarily sexual) relationships with women friends. Deborah felt that she had come up from the desert, the inner emotional deadness that made her life meaningless: "Now I know that I can't always be in touch with my feelings", she said, "but I don't feel an emotional cripple any more."

Discussion

My focus here is on the difficulties in the analytic treatment of analysands whose physical and psychic existence is in danger. For such analysands, it is as if life itself, in every casual and significant aspect, had come to seem perilous. Usually, their network of defences and transferences originated so far back in their life histories that they seem virtually constitutional.

Eissler's (1950, 1953) work with adolescent delinquents and schizophrenics led him to conclude that analytic technique, in any of its then usual ego psychological forms, might not be suitable for such cases. Eissler (1953) considered the ego of these analysands to be "modified"—that is, to have departed from a hypothetical, normal, ego organization and mode of functioning. Eissler's thinking on this matter was closely tied to Freud's "Analysis Terminable and Interminable" (1937c). In that paper, using his relatively new structural theory, Freud had proposed the idea of the modified or "altered ego". An "altered ego" is not fully available to the analytic method; it cannot "guarantee unshakeable loyalty to the work of analysis" (p. 239). Interpretation alone may culminate in a strengthening of defences.

In the same trend, in his well-known paper "The Effect of the Structure of the Ego on Psychoanalytic Technique", Eissler (1953) suggested that at times it is necessary to make major departures from interpretation only. He advised that, in the interest of their ultimate therapeutic goals, analysts should make sparing use of these departures, which he called "parameters", and only when they can anticipate analysing their non-analytic effects later on.

Eissler's important contribution consists in his view that it is often necessary for the analyst to be un-analytically interventionist in order to bring some analysands to be less terrified in facing their inner conflicts, so that—at least some of the time—they can understand and use interpretation for what it is, as an aid to beneficial change.

Psychoanalytic thought today is more experience-centred than it was in the 1950s, and it therefore expresses the matter of inaccessibility in a different way. Schafer (1997) states:

> To the extent that the ego is altered, it will experience interpretation as yet another version of old dangers, this is a version that threatens to bring about another traumatic overstimulation or deprivation, another seduction, punishment, exposure to guilt, humiliation or collapse of self-esteem, if not annihilation of the self itself. A steady diet of interpretation must therefore be experienced by the altered ego as one or another kind of tyranny. [p. 227]

The case study presented above shows the great difficulties I had in the treatment of a patient who, to my mind, can best be classified as the kind of very disturbed hysteric described by Zetzel (1968). What Deborah demanded from me was to repeat in treatment her infantile traumata (to exploit her sexually), regarding this as an absolute necessity for saving her life. My attempts to help her understand this and to confront her with the cruel and hostile way in which she treated me failed, because, as she suffered from a kind of "malignant narcissism"

(Kernberg, 1992), she experienced all references to our relationship as humiliating and persecutory.

Since the most decisive factor influencing the patient's experience of the analyst's interpretations is the current status of the transference, I tried to shift the transference constellation that developed in an adversarial way. For this purpose, I used a parameter—a "holding interpretation" (Kogan, 1995, 1997)—which was completely different in its form and content from interpretations encoded in a manner characteristic of analysis. By a "holding interpretation", I mean an intervention that conveyed to her not only the fact that I was in touch with her deepest anxieties, but, like the mother who holds the baby in her arms, it conveyed a soothing, life-giving embrace.

The decision to use this particular form of "holding", which included a verbal response to her need for love, stemmed from my fear when faced with my patient's implicit threat of suicide in situations in which this need was frustrated. When the negative transference culminated in her threat to leave treatment, I was aware of the implicit possibility of her becoming self-destructive if I did not acquiesce in some way. (My fear could be seen as a sign—effected by means of projective identification—of the gradual emergence of the patient's chronic traumatic state, the legacy of sexual overstimulation in childhood).

I had, therefore, to take another course of action. I had to become an emotional surrogate, to offer her emotions, in order to enable her to feel. For this purpose, it was not enough to use an "objective" interpretation (Gedo, 1994), which named in a kind of objective and neutral way the feelings evoked towards me in the transference (with or without linking them to emotions towards primary objects in the past). Instead, I had to "embody" the affective states by expressing them myself. Similarly to Modell's (1990) observation that in special moments in treatment it is virtually impossible to discern whether a specific insight originated with the analyst or with the analysand, these affective states could originate in her as well as in me.

In contrast to my former interpretations, which stressed my separate existence as an Other in the transference, I here assumed the role of a voice in the patient's own psychic universe.

Only by delineating the voice, which expressed her (or my) longing for love, could she become aware of the cruel and depriving way that she had treated me hitherto.

By becoming her emotional surrogate, I made myself available to a new object relationship that facilitated some understanding and growth. Loewald (1960) describes this process in the following way: "We know from analytic, as well as from life experience, that new spurts of self-development may be intimately connected with such 'regressive' rediscoveries of oneself, as may occur through the establishment of new object-relationships" (pp. 224–225).

I also believe that by becoming my patient's emotional surrogate, I responded intuitively to her regressive need for "primary love" (Balint, 1968) from a primary object. Anzieu (1986) expressed this eloquently:

> It is only through his discourse that the analyst can touch his patient. Through the internal view of elaborating an interpretation, the analyst has to find words that are symbolic equivalents of what was missing in the tactile exchanges between the baby and the mother. Through these words, which involve the body of the psychoanalyst speaking on a prelinguistic level, one can in fact touch the body of the patient. [p. 86]

Since her demand for further gratification stopped after I met her need verbally, I could conclude that my response was necessary to turn the process that started in a malign form of regression—the craving for satisfaction—into a benign one—a "regression for recognition" (Balint, 1968). By this I mean that Deborah was able to use my reaction to continue her internal dialogue.

The intervention described here included two sentences: the first addressed the patient in a simple, concrete, direct way, asking her not to leave treatment. The second took the form of a verse from poetry—it was metaphorical, affect-laden, and dramatic. It shared the need for love existing in patient and analyst alike. I believe that my statement conveyed a clear emotional message, and the tone of my voice—impregnated with emotions that embodied my words—enhanced its impact. It is possible that my words and the way they were spoken functioned as a "sonorous bath" (Lecourt, 1990), creating an association between touch and hearing. In contrast to insight, which is the result of a correct interpretation, this "holding interpretation" resulted in a feeling. While insight correlates with seeing, feeling correlates with touching. It was only through this emotional "touching" that the patient could begin to feel.

It is possible that under Deborah's unconscious wish to show me her vagina and to look at mine was a deeper need for a mutual relationship in which she had to "touch" my feelings in order to become in touch with her own.

Deborah did not give up her homosexual identity. She continued to feel attracted to women, but she gained enough respect for reality to stop her frantic search for a homosexual relationship whose purpose was to mask her inner emotional deadness.

In her interesting paper "Womanliness as a Masquerade", Riviere (1929) claims that "what appears as homosexual or heterosexual character-traits, or sexual manifestations, is the end result of the interplay of conflicts and not necessarily evidence of a radical or fundamental tendency. The difference between homosexual and heterosexual development results from differences in the degree of anxiety" (p. 303). It is possible, in this case, that the frantic search for a homosexual partner stopped because Deborah was better able to deal with her anxiety.

An important change occurred with the diminishment of her self-destructive, ego-alien tendencies, which stemmed from her interminable emotional frustration. This resulted from Deborah's working through her conflicting attitude towards her maternal introject—the "dead mother" (Green, 1986)—who, being herself tremendously threatened by emotions, prohibited the emotional life of the daughter. Deborah had to part from this castrated, as well as castrating, maternal imago so that she could become emotionally alive.

Many questions and doubts preoccupied me concerning the partial results of this treatment: What can we hope from psychoanalysis in cases in which homosexuality serves as a "manic defence" (Klein, Heimann, Isaacs, & Riviere, 1952; Winnicott, 1935) against fragmentation and psychic death? And what is the analyst's role in these cases? Should the analyst struggle against this defence, which may be experienced by patients as vital for their precarious psychic survival? Or should the analyst bring patients on the way to self-discovery, which may or may not lead them to giving up their homosexual life?

I do not presume to have the answers to these difficult questions. I only know that, though far from solving all her problems, Deborah emerged from the treatment better equipped to face life, as well as to face her homosexual conflict.

REFERENCES

Alden, L. E., Wiggins, J. S., & Pincus, A. L. (1990). Construction of circumflex scales for the inventory of interpersonal problems. *Journal of Personality Assessment, 55*: 521–536.

Anzieu, D. (1986). *Un peau pour les pensées. Entretiens avec Gilbert Tarab.* Paris: Clancier-Guenod.

Aisenstein, M. (1991). Entre psychanalyse et guérison. *Revue française de psychanalyse, 3.*

Balint, M. (1968). *The Basic Fault.* London & New York: Tavistock Publications, 1986.

Bateman, A. (1995). The treatment of borderline patients in a day hospital setting. *Psychoanalytic Psychotherapy, 9*: 3-16.

Beck, A., Ward, C. H., Mendelson, M., Mock, J., & Erlbaugh, J. (1961). An inventory for measuring depression. *Archives of General Psychiatry.*

Bion, W. (1959). Attacks on linking. *International Journal of Psycho-Analysis, 40*: 308–315.

Bion, W. (1962). A theory of thinking. *International Journal of Psycho-Analysis, 43*: 306–310.

Bion, W. (1967). *Second Thoughts*. London: Karnac Books, 1984.

Biswanger, L. (1947). *Ausgewählte Vorträge und Aufsätze*. Bern: Franke.

Chused, J. F. (1991). The evocative power of enactments. *Journal of the American Psychoanalytic Association, 39*: 615–640.

Cooper, P., Osborn, M., Gath, D., & Feggetter, G. (1982). Evaluation of a modified self-report measure of social adjustment. *British Journal of Psychiatry, 141*: 68–75.

Dejours, C. (1994). *Somatisation, psychanalyse et sciences du vivant*. Paris: Eshel.

Derogatis, L. R. (1983). *SCL–90R: Administration, Scoring and Procedures—Manual II*. Towson, MD: Clinical Psychometric Research.

Eissler, K. R. (1950). Ego psychological implications of the psychoanalytic treatment of delinquents. *Psychoanalytic Study of the Child, 5*: 97–121.

Eissler, K. R. (1953). The effect of the structure of the ego on psychoanalytic technique. *Journal of the American Psychoanalytic Association, 1*: 104–143.

Fain, M. (1982). *Le désir de l'interpréte*. Paris: Ed. Aubier Montaigne.

Fonagy, P. (1991). Thinking about thinking: some clinical and theoretical considerations in the treatment of a borderline patient. *International Journal of Psycho-Analysis, 72*: 639–656.

Freud, S. (1891). *On Aphasia*. New York: International Universities Press.

Freud, S. (1910i). The psycho-analytic view of psychogenic disturbance of vision. *S.E.*, 11.

Freud, S. (1914b). The Moses of Michelangelo. *S.E.*, 13.

Freud, S. (1914c). On narcissism: an introduction. *S.E.* 14.

Freud, S. (1920g). *Beyond the Pleasure Principle. S.E.* 18.

Freud, S. (1921c). *Group Psychology and the Analysis of the Ego. S.E.*, 18.

Freud, S. (1923b). *The Ego and the Id. S.E.*, 19.

Freud, S. (1933a). *New Introductory Lectures on Psycho-Analysis*. Lecture 31, *S.E.*, 22.

Freud, S. (1937c). Analysis terminable and indeterminable. *S.E.*, 23.

Freud, S. (1940a [1938]). *An Outline of Psycho-Analysis. S.E.*, 23.

Fromm-Reichmann, F. (1955). Clinical significance of intuitive process of the psychoanalyst. *Journal of the American Psychoanalytic Association, 3*: 82–88.

Gedo, J. E. (1994). Analytic interventions: the question of form. In: A. K. Richards & A. D. Richards (Eds.), *The Spectrum of Psychoanalysis: Essays in Honor of Martin S. Bergmann.* (pp. 111–129). Madison, CT: International Universities Press.

Green, A. (1986). The dead mother. In: *On Private Madness.* London: Hogarth Press.

Grinberg, L. (1990). Projective counteridentification. In: *The Goals of Psychoanalysis: Identification, Identity, and Supervision* (pp. 141–173). London: Karnac Books.

Grotstein, J. (1981). *Splitting and Projective Identification.* New York: Jason Aronson.

Gunderson, J. G., Frank, A. F., Ronningstam, E. F., Wachter, S., Lynch, V. J., & Wolf, P. J. (1989). Early discontinuance of borderline patients from psychotherapy. *Journal of Nervous and Mental Disease; 177*: 38–42.

Gunderson, J. G., Kolb, K., & Austin, V. (1981). The diagnostic interview for borderline patients. *American Journal of Psychiatry, 138*: 896–903.

Hartocollis, P. (1987). Current status of the diagnosis of borderline syndrome. In: F. Flach (Ed.), *Diagnostics and Psychopathology* (pp. 197–206). New York: W. W. Norton.

Heimann, P. (1952). Preliminary notes on some defense mechanisms in paranoid estates. *International Journal of Psycho-Analysis, 33*: 208–212.

Horowitz, L. M., Rosenbery, S. E., Baer, B. A., Ureno, G., & Villasenor, V. S. (1988). Inventory of interpersonal problems: psychometric properties and clinical applications. *Journal of Consulting and Clinical Psychology, 56*: 885–892.

Jacobs, T. (1993). The inner experiences of the analyst: their contribution to the analytic process. *International Journal of Psycho-Analysis, 74*: 7–14.

Johan, M. (1992). Panel. Enactments in psychoanalysis. *Journal of the American Psychoanalytic Association, 40*: 827–841.

Kernberg, O. F. (1975). *Borderline Conditions and Pathological Narcissism.* New York: Jason Aronson.

Kernberg, O. F. (1992). "Psychoanalytic Psychotherapy with Borderline Patients." Paper presented at University College London, Psychoanalysis Unit.

Klein, M. (1946). Notes on some schizoid mechanisms. *International Journal of Psychoanalysis, 27*: 99–110.

Klein, M., Heimann, P., Isaacs, S., & Riviere, J. (1952). *Developments in Psychoanalysis*. London: Hogarth Press.

Kogan, I. (1995). *The Cry of Mute Children—A Psychoanalytic Perspective of the Second Generation of the Holocaust*. London & New York: Free Association Books.

Kogan, I. (1997). The black hole of dread: the psychic reality of children of Holocaust survivors. In: J. Berke, S. Pierrides, A. Sabbaddini, & S. Schneider (Eds.), *Even Paranoids Have Enemies*. London & New York: Routledge.

Kohut, H. (1959). Introspection, empathy, and psychoanalysis. *Journal of the American Psychoanalytic Association, 7*: 459–483.

Kohut, H. (1971). *The Analysis of the Self*. New York: International Universities Press.

Kohut, H. (1977). *The Restoration of the Self*. New York: International Universities Press.

Lecourt, E. (1990). The musical envelope. In: D. Anzieu (Ed.), *Psychic Envelopes* (pp. 219–237). London: Karnac Books.

Loewald, H. W. (1960). On the therapeutic action of psychoanalysis. In: *Papers on Psychoanalysis*. New Haven, CT: Yale University Press, 1980.

Lopez-Corvo, R. E. (1992). About interpretation of self-envy. *International Journal of Psycho-Analysis, 73*: 719–728.

Lopez-Corvo, R. E. (1994). *Self Envy. Therapy and the Divided Inner World*. New York: Jason Aronson.

Marty, P. (1980). *L' ordre psychosomatique*. Paris: Payot.

Marty, P., de M'Uzan, M., & David, Ch. (1963). *L'investigation psychosomatique*. Paris: Presses Universitaires de France.

Mclaughlin, J. T. (1991). Clinical and theoretical aspects of enactment. *Journal of the American Psychoanalytic Association, 39*: 595–614.

Menninger, K. (1988). *Theory of Psychoanalytic Technique*. New York: Basic Books.

Modell, A. (1990). *Other Times, Other Realities*. Cambridge, MA: Harvard University Press.

Norton, K., & Hinshelwood, R. D. (1996). Severe personality disorder: treatment issues and selection for in-patient psychotherapy. *British Journal of Psychiatry, 168*: 723–731.

Ogden, T. (1994). *Subjects of Analysis*. Northvale, NJ: Jason Aronson; London: Karnac Books.

Ogden, T. (1997). Reverie and interpretation. *Psychoanalytic Quarterly, 66*: 567–595.

Pigman, G. W. (1995). Freud and the history of empathy. *International Journal of Psycho-Analysis, 76*: 237–256.

Potamianou, A. (1997). *Hope: A Shield in the Economy of Borderline States*. London: Routledge. [First published as *Un bouclier dans l'économie des états-limites*. Paris: Presses Universitaires de France, 1992.]

Potamianou, A. (1994). Réflexions sur les processus disinvestissants. *Revue Française de Psychosomatique, 5*: 101–105.

Riviere, J. (1929). Womanliness as a masquerade. *International Journal of Psycho-Analysis, 10*: 303–313.

Rosenberg, B. (1991). *Masochisme mortifure et masochisme gardien de la vie*. Paris: Presses Universitaires de France.

Roughton, R. E. (1993). Useful aspects of acting out: repetition, enactment, and actualization. *Journal of the American Psychoanalytic Association, 41*: 443–472.

Sandler, J. (1976a). Actualisation and object relationships, *Journal of the Philadelphia Association of Psychoanalysis, 3*: 59–70.

Sandler, J. (1976b). Countertransference and role responsiveness. *International Review of Psychoanalysis 3*: 43–47.

Schafer, R. (1997). *Tradition and Change in Psychoanalysis*. London: Karnac Books.

Sifneos, P. (1974). Reconsiderations of psychodynamic mechanisms in psychosomatic symptom formation. *Psychotherapy and Psychosomatics, 24*: 151–155.

Soloff, P. H. (1998). Algorithms for psychopharmacological treatment of personality dimensions: symptom-specific treatments for cognitive-perceptual, affective, and impulsive-behavioural dysregulation. *Bulletin of the Menninger Clinic, 62*: 195–214.

Spielberger, C. D., Gorsuch, R. L., & Lushene, R. E. (1970). *The State–Trait Anxiety Inventory (Self-Evaluation Questionnaire)*. Palo Alto, CA: Consulting Psychologists Press.

Vergopoulo, T. (Reporter) (1996). Panel: Bion's contribution to psychoanalytic theory and technique. Thirty-ninth Congress of the IPA, 1995. *International Journal of Psycho-Analysis, 77*: 575–577.

Waldinger, R. J., & Gunderson, J. G. (1984). Completed therapies with borderline patients. *American Journal of Psychiatry, 38*: 190–202.

Winnicott, D. W. (1935). The manic defence. In: *Collected Papers*. New York: Basic Books, 1958.

Winnicott, D. W. (1960). Ego distortion in terms of true and false self. In: *Maturational Processes and the Facilitating Environment*. New York: International Universities Press, 1966.

Winnicott, D. W. (1971). *Playing and Reality*. London: Tavistock.

Wolff, H. H. (1971). The therapeutic and developmental functions of psychotherapy. *British Journal of Medical Psychology, 44*: 117–130.

Zetzel, E. (1968). The true good hysteric. *International Journal of Psycho-Analysis, 49*: 256.

INDEX